*"Reading this book will undoubtedly make you a better rider.
It's insightful and packed with valuable tips.
I feel more confident about riding, having read it.
It may just save my life someday."*

— KERRY IN COLORADO

"I've always found David's books stimulating and educational."

— CHRIS IN WRIGHTSTOWN, PENNSYLVANIA

*"Riders who practice the suggestions in 'Motorcycle Hacks' are almost
guaranteed to be less likely to crash. It's nicely illustrated, with important
ideas explained clearly and repeatedly. It contains rider wisdom not found
in other publications. This book will definitely save lives."*

— MARK, MOTORCYCLE OWNER AND RIDER

*"I like the varied pace David used of short chapters and long chapters.
If you liked 'Motorcycle Smarts' and 'Motorcycle Dream Ride,' you'll
definitely like this book. Thanks!"*

— JOHN IN TEXAS

*"David explains lowside and highside crashes, unlike anything I've ever
seen. Even more importantly, he explains what triggers them and how you
can virtually eliminate them. David has a passion for explaining
motorcycles his way—and you can tell."*

— DONNA IN KENTUCKY

"Reading this book felt like I was talking to David over coffee."

— DAN IN SAN DIEGO, CALIFORNIA

MOTORCYCLE HACKS

Also by David Mixson

Motorcycle Smarts: Overcome Fear, Learn Control, Master Riding Well

(Book 1 in the 'Motorcycle Smarts' Book Series)

Motorcycle Dream Ride: My Alabama to Alaska Adventure

(Book 2 in the 'Motorcycle Smarts' Book Series)

Motorcycle Hacks

Everything My Motorcycle Mentors Taught Me
—and More

David Mixson

Copyright and Disclaimers

Motorcycle Hacks: Everything My Motorcycle Mentors Taught Me—and More

Copyright © 2023 by David Mixson

<u>motorcyclesmarts.com</u>

Disclaimer

Laws and Regulations

ISBN 978-1-7324532-7-2 (ebook)

ISBN 978-1-7324532-8-9 (paperback)

To Fred and Pete
for being my motorcycle mentors.

We make a living by what we get.
We make a life by what we give.
— Winston Churchill

———————

Contents

Part Three: Crash Avoidance Hacks

Part Four: Riding Gear Hacks

Warning

Every time I suit up to ride, I weigh my options and evaluate my risks. As long as the pleasure of riding overshadows the additional exposure, I'll continue to throw a leg over and strap on my helmet.

When it doesn't, I'll stop riding.

The risks are real. Motorcycle crashes—sometimes caused by negligent drivers—can cause serious injuries, even death.

In this book, I attempt to present accurate information that will ultimately make you a safer rider. But I'm human. My advice may not apply to every rider in every situation.

No book, including this one, can teach you how to ride a motorcycle proficiently. Please seek lessons from a licensed instructor.

Ride safely and at your own risk.

And while I'm at it, I might as well warn you that I'm bound to say something here that bothers you.

I like motorcycles with ABS, full face helmets, bright riding gear, and earplugs. I'm going to encourage you to avoid riding in groups, to think twice about riding at night, and to put off buying the brand-new GPS navigation system until next year.

BUT I CAN'T MAKE YOU DO ANY OF THIS—
AND THAT'S THE WAY I WANT IT.

If you want a Harley, buy one. If earplugs give you a headache, don't use them. If you want to ride without a helmet, that's your call.

More than anything, I want you to know that you can reduce your chances of crashing by making good decisions and taking an active role in improving your riding skills.

Can you reduce your risks to zero? Absolutely not.

But you CAN change the odds of crashing.

 In the end, if you adopt just some of the suggestions I present, I've accomplished what I set out to do—which is exactly what my motorcycle mentors did for me.

Thanks for following along.

Foreword

By Drew Mixson

THE AUTHOR'S FAVORITE SON

I love it when friends ask me what my dad's into.

I usually reply with something like this. "Well, he's an engineer for NASA, super into bourbon, and rides a motorcycle."

Funny enough, it isn't working for NASA that grabs people's interest. The follow-up question is almost always in regard to *motorcycles*.

It gets even better when I tell them he's ridden to Alaska.

"Wait, he rode his motorcycle to Alaska?"

"And back," I say with a slight smile.

This raises eyebrows first and foremost because we live in Alabama —and Alaska is a long way from home.

When my dad dives into something, he goes all in and studies it. Any advice he gives is well-researched and tested.

He isn't just spitballing. He's done his homework.

That much I know.

Introduction

The concept for this book came at 9:22 p.m. on a Wednesday evening while I was out of town working on another book project.

After an amazing day of writing, I poured myself a bourbon (neat) and pulled out Seth Godin's book *Poke the Box*.

If you know much about Godin's work, you know that many of his books are short. *Poke the Box* is one of his shortest—exactly as long as it needs to be and not a single page longer.

Even though authors are supposed to finish one book before they start another, I couldn't help myself. I immediately pulled out a white sheet of printer paper and started jotting down ideas.

In the margin of my hand-written notes, I wrote:

I WANT TO WRITE A BOOK SO CONCISE THAT A RIDER CAN SIT DOWN IN ONE SITTING AND LEARN SOMETHING THAT COULD SAVE THEIR LIFE.

The most popular motorcycle skills mega-books miss this mark.

They're too long and too general. Authors spend too much time on fluffy topics (like how to enjoy Sturgis) and too little on the important ones (like what riders have consistently been doing wrong for decades that triggers most *lowside* and *highside* crashes).

I wanted to write something that was concise—that mattered.

Two men spent a considerable amount of time mentoring me when I first started riding a motorcycle. They nurtured my passion for learning how motorcycles work.

I studied everything I could find and practiced what I learned.

Their guidance was less about giving me the correct answers to my questions and more about guiding me to my own conclusions.

I write books about motorcycles to pay that forward.

Motorcycle Hacks is the third book in the *Motorcycle Smarts* book series, and it's broken into seven main sections:

PART ONE introduces the importance of having the right *mindset*. Nothing good happens on a motorcycle unless you get this part right.

PART TWO introduces some of the *riding hacks* my mentors shared with me and some that I learned for myself along the way. Be forewarned. These are all over the board—from my thoughts on riding in a group to trying to convince you NOT to ride a motorcycle.

PART THREE unpacks *lowside and highside crashes*—and the electronics that can keep riders from crashing. Understanding lowside and highside crashes (and what triggers them) isn't all that difficult.

The amazing thing about these crashes is that they're avoidable— yet, they're HARDLY MENTIONED IN OTHER BOOKS.

Consider this as a bonus section of sorts because I explained these crashes in even more depth in *Motorcycle Smarts*. I included them here because I promised myself I would explain them in every motorcycle skills book I wrote. They're too important not to.

PART FOUR explores some tips and tricks about *riding gear*. When I started riding, I was slow to embrace gear made for motorcyclists. Who knew riding a motorcycle didn't have to be painful?

PART FIVE covers a variety of *how-to hacks*. Here, I'll discuss tips like how to find neutral and how to handle a bike that won't start.

PART SIX defines more *riding tips* I've discovered along the way. This section is another brain dump of the hacks I had in my pile of notes that didn't make it into *Motorcycle Smarts*.

PART SEVEN has a few *closing thoughts* and a personal challenge.

And finally, in the APPENDIX, I introduce my motorcycle mentors, give a sneak peek of other books in the *Motorcycle Smarts* series, and share what listeners have said about the *Motorcycle Mentor Podcast*.

As a bonus, I've added several chapters on more lighthearted topics and sprinkled them throughout the book to give the reader a break.

Who Should Read This Book?

This book isn't just for riders starting out. It's for riders who are receptive to learning new things—even though they've ridden for decades. It's for riders who give a damn about their riding safety.

If you've been riding for long, some of the tips I write about won't be new concepts to you. My hope, however, is that *every* reader will pick up something new they can use to enjoy the sport more safely.

You might NOT like what I have to say.

To get the most out of this book, you'll need to be open to the idea that some of the things you've learned about motorcycles aren't correct.

If you think you're fine because you wear a helmet, think again.

If *loud pipes save lives* is your primary safety strategy, you're really not going to like everything I have to say about them.

Oh yeah. And if your hand grips are way over your head, this book probably isn't for you either—mostly because the physics of choppers is different than normal motorcycles.

My goal isn't for you to agree with everything I profess.

If I say something that bothers you, know that I'm only saying it because I believe it could help *one* rider. I certainly didn't do this series to get rich. At $3/copy (or whatever it works out to be), I'll never get to minimum wage for the time spent writing and editing it.

But that was never my goal—or my purpose.

It's also probably worth mentioning what you won't find here.

In these pages, I won't be talking about how to select riding gear or get the most out of your next biker rally.

MASTERING THE ART OF RIDING A MOTORCYCLE WELL is about learning how to ride the right way. It's about taking each ride seriously and making good decisions based on the laws of physics.

It's about being confident that you can avoid distracted drivers. It's about having a plan before you need a plan. It takes effort.

It's about having the head knowledge of how your motorcycle works so you can make it go where you want it to go. It's about understanding why riders crash.

And There's More

As you can see from the length of this book, I had more to say than I originally thought. When I got home from my writing trip, I gathered my notes that didn't make it into my first book, *Motorcycle Smarts,* and I had a pile of paper six inches tall.

At that moment, I realized this book would need to be longer than Godin's. Fortunately, I was able to keep some of the topics super short.

I hope this makes consuming it in short blocks of time easy—like the *Chicken Soup for the Soul* book series.

There's one last thing I need to warn you about.

I call the thing I write about in this book a *motorcycle* and a *bike*.

I mostly blame my riding buddy (and friend) Mike for teaching me this. I found it strange the first hundred or so times he referred to his motorcycle as a bike. It wasn't long before I started doing the same.

My parents were right.

You *are* influenced by the people you hang out with.

Back in 2007, I invited my mentors to my house for an evening of motorcycle talk in my basement. After a few minutes of light conversation, I pulled out a stack of notes, looked them in the eyes, and said:

"Someday, I want to explain motorcycles my way."

THIS BOOK IS A PART OF THAT VISION.

You're in the right place, and I'm thrilled you're here!

A Fresh Approach

Every study on motorcycle crashes I've seen says the same thing:

Riders are making the same mistakes we did decades ago—even with mandatory training and plenty of books on the subject.

An NHTSA study in *2012* found that motorcyclists were 26 times more likely than car occupants to die in accidents (per mile traveled).[1] A similar NHTSA study in *2018* showed that riders are now 28 times more likely to die in motor vehicle traffic crashes.[2]

In *Motorcycle Smarts*, I dissected the Hurt Report, a crash investigation study conducted forty years ago. In this book, I'll take a look at a crash study done more recently.

I'll go into more detail about the study a little later—but suffice it to say, nothing seems to have changed.

What we're doing to educate riders isn't working.

We need a fresh approach.

The *Motorcycle Smarts* book series is my attempt to do that.

The foundation of every book I've written on motorcycles begins with a core belief that every rider can change their chances of crashing.

My passion has never wavered, and I doubt it ever will.

The real issue isn't that riders get banged up when they crash. That's a given. It's that average riders crash by themselves way too often making the same mistakes riders did generations ago.

Average riders use their rear brake way too much, don't know what lowside crashes are (and what causes them), and say there's little they can do to keep from crashing—thinking, *when my time comes, it comes.*

Average riders make errors that account for half of all crashes, don't know how to react when a driver makes a mistake, and choose whether to wear a helmet based on whether their riding buddies wear one.

Average riders consider fashion over function way too often.

Average riders do the same things average riders did decades ago.

Don't fall into the trap of thinking the way to have riders crash less is to make them wear helmets. Helmets don't keep us from crashing.

I don't care what you wear or what you ride. I care that you understand how motorcycles work so you can master why they crash. Once you do this, you can avoid triggering some of the most common types of crashes—and maybe even outlive your riding buddies.

It's time for a fresh approach to explaining how motorcycles work and how they crash—so a wife won't be left without her husband, a husband without his wife, or a child without their parent.

Something's not working.
We need a fresh approach.

Part One: Mindset Hacks

Being the best rider you can be starts with having the right mindset.

Mindset is the motivation that fuels action—and a good mindset starts with taking ownership of your safety.

In this section, I'll share what taking ownership of *my* riding safety means to me. I'll also spell out what I believe about motorcycles.

ONE

Pinned Against a Wall

"A forty-year-old man was pinned against the wall while attempting to put his motorcycle on the center stand for the first time. His wife found him unconscious several days later."

I don't need a spotter, I thought. I'm an engineer.

Seconds later, I was in trouble.

Before I knew it, my bike came over on me and threw me against the wall like I was nothing. My new (used) motorcycle wasn't looking as good as she did when I purchased her three days before.

I wondered for a brief moment how it happened so quickly. But I realized my life hung in the balance and that I had better take action quickly if I wanted to survive.

Nobody was within shouting range except my dog.

The handlebars were pushing against my ribcage. My feet were in an awkward position against a stack of empty clay pots.

I figured I had one (maybe two) tries to push the motorcycle off of me before I made the next day's news.

I took a deep breath, which hurt because my ribs were injured, and pushed with everything I had. Nothing meaningful happened.

On the second attempt, I repositioned my legs to get better footing. I was getting tired and knew I needed this attempt to work.

I said a quick prayer for strength, then pushed as hard as I could.

And it worked!

I quickly put the side stand down (no more center stand for me until I get a spotter) and allowed the motorcycle to rest on it.

The pain came later.

Thankful to be alive, I smiled and wondered how many people had done the exact same thing.

Later that evening, I told my wife what had happened.

It didn't sound nearly as exciting as it felt in real-time. She knew the punch line that I survived and was fine.

It wasn't until three days later that my doctor
informed me I had broken two ribs.

TWO

Use Your Front Brake

Every crash study I've devoured said the same thing—motorcycles stop faster and more predictably when riders use their front brake.

Yet many riders ignore the data and think they're smarter.

I imagine their ignorance might be is rooted in the memories they had as kids when they used their front brake on a bicycle and were launched over the handlebars. But motorcycles aren't bicycles.

The draft version of this book had a comprehensive list of study after study showing how using your front brake was superior. I deleted all that because it seemed so intense. Here's the condensed version.

If you don't use your front brake, it's going to take you a lot farther to stop than me—when it matters the most.

It's no accident that I put this as the first real chapter in this book. The myth that your front brake is dangerous needs to be tossed out in the trash and buried. Once and for all.

Hey. One more thing.

Have you heard about the 'Motorcycle Smarts' Quick Tips Newsletter? It's where I share some of my best riding tips. Sign up at the link below. Unsubscribe at any time.

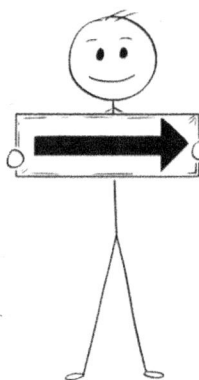

"Motorcycle Smarts" Quick Tips Newsletter

Free weekly riding tips you can consume in less than 3 minutes— delivered to your inbox for you to use and share with others.

motorcyclesmarts.com/tips

You're not doing everything you can to keep from crashing until you're signed up.

---

motorcyclesmarts.com/tips

THREE

Take Ownership of Your Safety

It's hard for me to understand this, but some riders don't think they can reduce their chances of crashing. Instead of taking responsibility for riding better *offensively* (by improving their riding skills) and *defensively* (by looking out for the other guy), they place their faith in mathematical statistics and believe:

"When my time comes, it comes."

Don't fall into the trap of thinking this way!

Here are six things you can do to ride more safely.

1. Taking ownership of your riding safety is about believing you can reduce your risk of crashing.

MUCH OF WHAT I WRITE ABOUT IS TO SHOW RIDERS THEY CAN CHANGE THEIR CHANCES OF CRASHING.

Making this affirmation is the most important step in your journey to MASTERING THE ART OF RIDING WELL. There's no motivation to take action if you don't believe your actions will influence the outcome.

I realize that I'll have to convince some of you.

I'll do this by unpacking how motorcycles work, explaining how to avoid certain types of crashes caused by rider error, highlighting what the Hurt Report teaches us about why riders crash, and by deciphering motorcycle electronics that can eliminate certain types of crashes.

2. TAKING OWNERSHIP OF YOUR RIDING SAFETY IS ABOUT UNDERSTANDING HOW TO CONTROL YOUR MOTORCYCLE.

And the foundation for understanding how to control your motorcycle is *head knowledge.* Understand how countersteering works so you can use it to make your motorcycle go where you want it to go. Understand lowside and highside crashes (and what causes them) so you can avoid them. Understand how to use your brakes so you can stop faster.

3. TAKING OWNERSHIP OF YOUR RIDING SAFETY IS ABOUT IMPROVING YOUR DEFENSIVE RIDING SKILLS.

I've avoided crashing on numerous occasions by anticipating what motorists might do. Like the time I was riding on I-65 heading north toward Nashville, Tennessee. I was in the right lane, and a motorist in the left lane shot across in front of me to make the exit ramp.

I had just slowed down, so I wasn't beside him, just in case.

Anticipate where drivers might want to go and be somewhere else.

4. TAKING OWNERSHIP OF YOUR RIDING SAFETY IS ABOUT IMPROVING YOUR OFFENSIVE RIDING SKILLS.

One of the best ways to do this is to take a hands-on training class. No book (including this one), training video, or Internet search can substitute for hands-on instruction.

Rider coaches are worth their weight in gold. Let them help you.

5. TAKING OWNERSHIP OF YOUR RIDING SAFETY IS ABOUT CONSTANTLY IMPROVING.

The best riders I know say they *never stop learning*. Before and after every ride, think about what you need to work on. Better yet, write your thoughts in a journal so you can monitor your progress.

6. TAKING OWNERSHIP OF YOUR RIDING SAFETY IS ABOUT
HAVING THE RIGHT MINDSET.

It's about engaging in the idea that you can always do more to get better. It's about staying interested long enough to read this book all the way through. It's about caring about your loved ones enough to take this stuff seriously. Here's the honest truth.

To be a better-than-average rider, you have to THINK DIFFERENTLY than average riders.

You need a different mindset.

Riding a motorcycle is tough. Riding a motorcycle well is tougher. Reading this book is a wonderful first move toward—
MASTERING THE ART OF RIDING WELL.

Congratulations. You're on the right track.
Let's keep going.

FOUR

What I Believe

Someone once left a review of my book *Motorcycle Dream Ride* and said I sounded arrogant because I had a BMW motorcycle.

What the reviewer doesn't know is that I drive a car with 470,000 miles on it and that I still have the same used BMW motorcycle I rode to Alaska seven years ago. That bike is now over fourteen years old.

To clear things up, I thought I would tell you what I believe.

First, I believe all riders are created equally.

I don't care if you ride a cruiser, tourer, adventure bike, sport bike, dirt bike, or scooter. To me, Hondas carry the same clout as Harleys, and Vespas are real motorcycles. I *do* think Ducatis are beautiful, but I *don't* think you're any better because you ride one.

The same goes for Harleys, BMWs, and Triumphs.

I believe most riders don't care what you wear or what you ride. I also believe that when you do encounter a jerk that acts like his stuff is better than your stuff, you should ignore him.

I believe all riders share a common bond and should wave to each other—regardless of what type of motorcycle each is riding.

I believe gear made for motorcyclists is more comfortable.

I also believe every rider should wear a helmet. But I'm not looking to get helmets mandated. That's your decision.

I believe motorcycles shouldn't be purchased when you have credit card debt or struggle to pay your power bill. First things first.

I believe men and women are equally qualified to ride.

I believe that you're never too old to start riding—as long as you're in good mental and physical condition.

I believe motorcycles break barriers. It doesn't matter where you work, how much you make, or what color your skin is.

When I see another rider, I see a friend.

And lastly, I believe motorcycles can be inherently dangerous, and that skilled riders crash and die every day when there was absolutely *nothing* they could have done to avoid it.

But I also believe that under-skilled riders crash and die every day when there WAS something they could have done to avoid it.

Every rider can reduce their risk of crashing.
I wrote the 'Motorcycle Smarts' book series to show you how.

FIVE

Nobody Wants to Kill You

Folks in cars don't want to kill us!

There's nothing you could say that would change my mind.

Thinking everybody is out to get you is unhealthy—and it could make you lose your cool when you need to keep it.

When I'm in a car, I'd rather crash into *anything* than someone on a motorcycle. I certainly don't want to live with that trauma.

And I think most people would agree.

Having said that, if you own a motorcycle for longer than a day, you're going to run across someone who does something stupid.

My best advice is to keep your cool.

When someone pulls into your space, stay calm. There's no reason for a temper tantrum. You're not in third grade anymore.

There's no need to catch up to the culprit and make hand gestures. There's no place for anger that might lead to bigger trouble.

Road rage is never a viable solution.

That's why I try to begin every ride with this mindset.

I don't believe for a second that ANYONE wants to run me over while I'm on a motorcycle.

The crash data is crystal clear. A significant percentage of multi-vehicle crashes is attributed to motorists not seeing us.

Are you doing everything you can to be visible?

I once rode with a good friend from work who had just purchased a motorcycle. He had ridden for most of his life but taken a few years off while his kids were young.

On our first ride together, a car pulled out right in front of us, and my friend flipped out. Before I could process what was happening, he took off after the automobile in a rage.

Seconds later, he pulled up next to the car and started yelling.

I couldn't hear what he was saying, but I'm confident it wasn't nice. His visor was up, and he was pointing his finger as he yelled at *her*.

I wanted to crawl inside a hole and hide.

At that moment, I decided I would never ride with him again.

A few months later, he told me he was selling his street motorcycle and going back to riding dirt bikes.

"I can't handle all the crazies riding so close to me."

I don't recall how I responded. But silently, I felt relieved.

I don't believe for a second that lady was out to kill us.

I just don't.
And neither should you.

Part Two: Riding Hacks

If you've read my other books or listened to my podcast, you know this already. I like to approach things from a different perspective.

I'm an engineer by training, and that's how I'm wired. I like taking complex concepts and breaking them down so I can understand them.

That's what I've tried to do throughout this book.

In this section, I'll share some riding tips my mentors shared with me—and ones I've picked up for myself along the way.

Some of them are short, standalone thoughts. Some are a bit more in-depth. Hopefully, this rhythm will make them easy to consume.

SIX

My First Ride With Fred

The first ride with my mentor was the most nerve-racking ride of my life—even worse than the time in Idaho (years later) when Mike and I got caught in a storm from hell on the way back from Alaska.

Mike and I thought we were goners that day.

I'd been riding for about four months when my mentor Fred asked me if I wanted to ride to a Trials motorcycle event two hours away.

My first thought was, "Oh crap. What if I do something stupid?"

I was nervous because he had spent so much time helping me get started. I didn't want him to see that curves were a problem for me.

I couldn't help but wonder how curvy the roads might be.

At his suggestion, we met for breakfast and proceeded from there. I was so sick with fear that I opted for black coffee only.

As we pulled away, I felt my heart racing. I knew there was a long list of things I could do to screw up this day.

If I do something stupid, I just hope I die really fast so I won't have to see the disappointment on his face.

The roads to the event were straight, and we made it fine.

If you've never seen a Trials event, look it up on YouTube. They're amazing. Better yet, attend an event in person.

As we were walking back to our bikes, Fred asked. "David, do you want to take a different route back that has more curves?"

"Sure," I whispered.

Oh my gosh, I've just been peer pressured into riding curves!

I knew my best option to survive the ride back was to ride in the back. Fred taught me that.

"Fred, I'll ride in the back so I can ride at my own pace."

He smiled like a proud parent. Perfect. If I die on the ride back, at least he'll know I listened to his mentoring.

The ride back was plastered with curves, and it took all the skills I had at the time to manage them.

Every time Fred went out of sight, he would pull off and wait for me—just as the best motorcycle mentor in the world should.

An hour or so later, we parted ways at the spot we met for breakfast. Fred took a left, and I continued straight toward home.

When Fred got out of sight, I breathed a sigh of relief, checked my drawers, and said a silent prayer of thanks inside my helmet that I had survived the day without doing something stupid.

A few days later, Fred asked how I liked the pace of our ride back.

"It was at the top end of my comfort zone," I said.

Fred paused for a second.

"Hum. I slowed my pace a lot to make sure you were okay."

I quickly changed the subject.

SEVEN

You Can Reduce Your Chances of Crashing

The foundation of everything I write about is the belief that riders can change their chances of crashing—and I think I'm right.

Everything I've seen in the crash studies suggests there are obvious trends to how riders before us have crashed. An easy example is that we increase our chances of crashing if we drink alcohol before we ride.

I've certainly never seen a study that suggests you are *less* likely to crash and die on a motorcycle if you get wasted before you ride.

Then, don't we *reduce* our chances of crashing if we don't drink?

From here, things get a little more complex.

One thing the crash studies all suggest is that motorists often hit us because they fail to see us. To me, this says that if I wear hi-vis yellow reflective gear I'm reducing my chances of crashing. Right?

Taking it a step further, if most all lowside and highside crashes are triggered by a locked-up rear tire (more on that later), wouldn't I be reducing my chances of crashing if I rode a motorcycle that had ABS?

Continuing, let's say the crash data suggests (and it does) that per-mile traveled riders are more likely to crash at night. If I avoided riding at night, wouldn't I be reducing my chances of crashing?

I could go on and on, but I think you get my point.

To say we can't change our chances of crashing and dying on a motorcycle is ABSURD.

If I didn't believe this, I wouldn't be typing these words at 1:21 a.m.
But I am.

EIGHT

Never Crash Alone

Crashing alone, as it pertains to this chapter, means you crash all by yourself because you made a rider error that caused it—you go wide in a turn, or lock up your rear tire and lowsided or highsided.

Crashing alone is referred to as a *single-vehicle accident* in the crash studies—and the percentage of single-vehicle crashes is staggering.

News flash. It doesn't have to be this way.

When I started riding, I made a promise to myself that I wouldn't crash by myself for one year. I figured I could control this. Right?

The concept was surprisingly empowering. It led me to make the mental connection that I *could* change my chances of crashing.

Instead of accepting the concept that I was just as likely as average riders to crash at any moment, I was determined to cut my chances by making sure I didn't do anything stupid. And I certainly didn't want to tell my mentors I messed up and crashed all by myself.

According to a 2001 NHTSA study, nearly half of all motorcycle accidents are single-vehicle crashes—where no other human, animal, or vehicle was involved in (or caused) the crash.[1]

Think about the power of this statistic until it sinks in.

Let me say it another way.

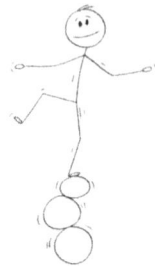

In nearly half of all motorcycle crashes, the rider crashed alone. And when riders crash alone, it's usually because they made an error and caused the crash.

Why doesn't every rider get excited about this data? It proves that we can reduce our risks by taking care of our own business.

Hogwash to those who say you can't change your odds of crashing. The data proves you are wrong.

Fifteen years later, I still have the same mindset I did back when I started. I make it a priority to do everything I can not to crash alone—and it starts with understanding *why* riders crash.

I challenge you to make the same commitment.

Will you do this?

Crashing alone is for the low-information rider who doesn't want to be bothered by the data that shows us how we're killing ourselves. Don't be a low-information rider.

NINE

All Motorcycles Depreciate

I've never been a fan of the hype that some bikes go up in value.

While there are exceptions to every rule, if Harley's appreciated on a consistent basis, I'd buy one every year and sell it one year later.

I contend that's not the case—at least not on a consistent basis.

And please, I don't want to hear about the *one* time you sold a used motorcycle for more than you paid for it new one year earlier.

The truth is those motorcycle manufacturers would love for you to believe the $25k motorcycle they're selling—that is twice as much as some other bikes in its class—is going to be worth more next year.

It's an effective sales tactic at best—a lie at worst.

Okay, maybe it's not always the case that motorcycles depreciate. It seems like I recall the guys on the TV show *Pickers* paying top dollar for vintage motorcycles. But that's only for a small group of bikes.

And who has 80 years to wait to cash in?

Just like expensive cars have the farthest to fall in value, expensive motorcycles have the same tendency to depreciate fast.

Be wary of the sales pitch that the thing they want you to buy is going to be worth more once you buy it. That rarely happens.

Now you know why I prefer to buy used motorcycles.

TEN

Countersteering

Countersteering is how you control your motorcycle.

In *Motorcycle Smarts*, I spent a great deal of time explaining countersteering. Here, I'll just cover the basics.

A textbook review of countersteering would require a discussion of a phenomenon known as gyroscopic precession. While this might be interesting to some, it's not important to understand the physics.

It's important to understand how countersteering gives us control.

MY SIMPLIFIED BUT JUST AS ACCURATE DEFINITION OF COUNTERSTEERING IS THE PHYSICS OF HOW YOU TURN YOUR MOTORCYCLE.

If you've taken a hands-on training course or read a motorcycle skills book, you've heard the phrase "push right to go right" and "push left to go left." This is countersteering. This is how you control your bike.

See Figure 10-1 (below).

Figure 10-1 Countersteering
(Push on Left Handlebar to Lean Left)

Sound Backwards?

You have probably noticed that countersteering is counterintuitive and *backward*. Pushing on the left handlebar is the same as turning (steering) the handlebar to the right. That's right, to initiate a turn you actually turn the handlebar in the *opposite* direction you want to go.

Let me say this again because I know it's hard to believe.

When you want to lean your motorcycle to the *left* (and turn left), you actually turn the handlebar to the *right* (which is the same input as pushing on the left handlebar).

This is true whether you realize it or not.

Isn't that amazing?

The motorcycle instructor gods of the past got it right when they crafted the slogan "push left to go left." They could have easily said, "turn right to go left," which is painfully confusing but equally correct.

If any of this sounds confusing, I understand. I struggled to make the mental connection of countersteering when I first started riding.

During my first MSF class, the instructor spent a great deal of time trying to get us to understand countersteering (with our head) and feel countersteering (with our body).

To do this, the instructor placed cones in a curve.

Then he had us ride around the curve faster and faster to force us to use countersteering to make the motorcycle turn in a tighter circle. The only way we could make the turn riding that fast was to push on the inside handlebar with purpose.

Over and over, the instructor called out, "Go faster. Make the bike lean more by pushing on the inside handlebar."

Countersteering didn't feel natural to me that day. My head didn't understand countersteering, and my body never made the connection. It wasn't until months later that countersteering made sense.

QUICK TIP: It's probably worth noting that countersteering doesn't start working until your wheels are rolling over a certain speed. There's passionate debate about the exact speed countersteering takes over. Some say countersteering starts working at about 15 mph. I say if your feet are comfortably up on the pegs, it's probably safe to assume that countersteering is hard at work.

Understanding Countersteering

Why do you need to understand countersteering with your head if you are using it already? You need to understand countersteering with your head so you can make your motorcycle go where you want it to go.

Countersteering is how you do normal turns.

Countersteering is how you dodge an object in the road.

It's what you use to make delicate adjustments in a sweeping turn. It's how you tighten a turn when you're running wide in a curve on a mountain pass, where death is a real possibility if you run off the road.

Countersteering is powerful, but it doesn't require much input. An 80-pound woman can make an 800-pound Goldwing lean instantly.

Curves are easier once you master countersteering.

Push on your right handlebar gently to make your motorcycle lean (turn) to the right. Push on your left handlebar gently to make it lean (turn) to the left. If you need to tighten your turn radius, simply push a little more on the inside handlebar, and your bike will lean more.

Feeling Countersteering for Yourself

Once you grasp countersteering with your head, it's time to feel it.

In a vacant parking lot, come up to about 20 mph and take your left hand off the handlebar. Next, use only your throttle hand to make the motorcycle turn. Notice how it leans to the right when you push on the handlebar with your right hand, and leans to the left when you pull back on the right handlebar?

Feel it? You're turning the handlebar in the opposite direction.

Hence the term COUNTERsteering.

Don't stop until you make the mental connection.

Don't stop until it becomes a part of your muscle memory. Only then will you be able to use it to make your motorcycle go where you want it to go during the stress of an emergency.

It wasn't until I made the connection of how countersteering works that I felt confident riding and confident that I could make my motorcycle go where I wanted it to go.

Countersteering is the physics that puts YOU in control of your motorcycle.

Powerful stuff.

ELEVEN

Read the Hurt Report

You probably know this by now, but the Hurt Report has shaped the way I ride more than any other motorcycle crash study.

Every rider who is even thinking about riding a motorcycle should read this report—at least the summary. It's easy to consume with practical recommendations that any rider can benefit from.

Yes, it was done in the 80s.

Yes, it is still relevant.

The information in the Hurt Report could save your life.

In *Motorcycle Smarts,* I unpacked my ten favorite findings from the Hurt Report and gave an analysis of how we can embrace each finding to reduce our chances of crashing.

Take a look at that, or at least search for the Hurt Report online. Its official title is:

Motorcycle Accident Cause Factors and Identification of Countermeasures Volume 1: Technical Report.[1]

The Hurt Report is packed with useful information. It reveals why we crash and shows us how we can avoid many of them.

Becoming a proficient rider begins with head knowledge.

I read the Hurt Report before I bought my first motorcycle. It gave me confidence that I could change my chances of crashing.

Reading it can change your chances of crashing too.

TWELVE

Friction 101

Warning: I'm about to discuss something I learned in physics back in college. I loved that class. *Roll your eyes here if you want.*

This is the one thing riders need to know about friction: The coefficient of *static* friction is greater than the coefficient of *kinetic* friction.

What this means is that a skidding tire has less stopping friction (mojo) than a tire that is still rolling but braking.

If you remember nothing else, remember this.

The fastest way to stop a motorcycle is to apply maximum braking WITHOUT LOCKING UP (skidding) your tires.

THIRTEEN

Myth: Motorcycles Save Money

I think it's funny when want-to-be-riders try to convince their loved ones that getting a motorcycle will save them money.

Owning a motorcycle isn't for the faint of heart. It will likely cause more stress than bliss in your relationships, and in most situations, it's going to end up being an expensive hobby.

Maybe not as bad as a boat, but possibly close.

It sounds palatable: better gas mileage (maybe), cheaper insurance (a possibility), and less maintenance (I'm not so sure). But the truth is owning a motorcycle will likely put a drain on your finances.

For most of us, it's impractical to get rid of our car when we buy a motorcycle. So the motorcycle will be an *additional* cost.

I suppose if you live in a big city with public transportation, you might be able to get by without a car. But if you have a house or kids, you'll struggle without something with four wheels. How will you take little Bobby to baseball practice or get ten bags of mulch?

Oh, your spouse owns a car?

If your spouse is a normal person, she'll tire quickly of managing the family taxi service by herself.

"Honey, after you take Bobby to baseball practice, would you pick up ten bags of mulch at Home Depot?"

"Sure thing. Is there anything else you need since you sold your car so you could buy a motorcycle?"

Yeah right?!

"BUT DAVE, I'LL SAVE MONEY ON GAS."

Here's what I discovered during my first year.

When I rode somewhere, I always took the long way to get there. In fact, on most occasions, I made up the destination so I would have a reason to ride somewhere. In other words, I wasn't going anywhere.

So, those miles couldn't really be tracked as savings because they were actually an additional expense. Nice try.

Want cheap transportation? Buy a used Honda Accord instead.

I had one with 300K miles that was reliable and inexpensive.

If you want a motorcycle, negotiate that as an additional purchase. Don't even start with the idea you'll buy a motorcycle to save money.

―――――――――

Because most of the time,
that's not going to happen.

FOURTEEN

Cars Turning Left Across Your Lane

One of my biggest takeaways from the Hurt Report is that riders can reduce their chances of crashing in so many ways.

One of the things that caught my attention most was that approximately 28 percent of multi-vehicle crashes involved a car turning left in front of (or into) a motorcyclist. See Figure 14-1 (below)

Knowing this tendency means we can do something about it.

During my first riding season and ever since, I've used this data to help me focus on *not* letting the same thing happen to me. Obviously, I can't eliminate the possibility, but I *can* take steps to reduce it.

I constantly scan for vehicles coming toward me that look like they might be planning to turn left across my lane. And when I see one, I assume that they don't see me and that they're going to proceed.

In every situation, I simply adjust my speed so if they do cross, I'll be able to avoid hitting them with more braking.

Some like the idea of flashing their headlights as a gesture to make sure they see you. I don't like that because it's confusing.

To me, when someone flashes their headlights at me, I usually take that to mean they're giving the okay to proceed—like when you flash your lights when an 18-wheeler passes you on an Interstate, and you're giving them the all-clear to pull back into your lane.

See Figure 14-1 (below)

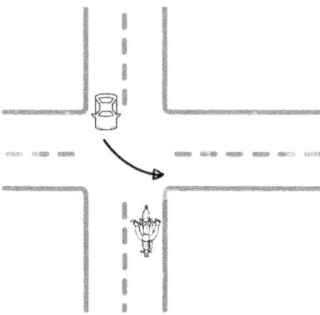

Figure 14-1 Motorists Turning Left Into Us

If motorcyclists could eliminate this one type of accident scenario, the crash data would change. Even if we could only reduce it by half (or a fourth), significantly fewer riders would die every year.

THIS DATA WAS A HUGE MOTIVATOR FOR ME WHEN I STARTED RIDING—AND IT CONTINUES TO BE SOMETHING I LOOK FOR EVERY SECOND I'M ON MY MOTORCYCLE.

And so can you.

FIFTEEN

Use Your Front Brake—The Data

This chapter is only for motorcycles designed by engineers. If you ride a chopper, skip ahead because the physics here probably doesn't apply.

Do choppers even have front brakes?

The first thing to know about normal on-street motorcycle braking is that you should mostly USE YOUR FRONT BRAKE.

Rider coaches know this, but somehow some riders still don't.

A ton of test data shows that 70 to 90 percent of a bike's stopping power comes from the front tire (front brake). This is because weight is transferred to the front of the motorcycle when you apply your brakes. When this happens, the front tire has more stopping power (friction), and the back tire has less. Pure physics.

It's the same way on a car. The front tires provide the vast majority of the stopping power. Have you ever driven with your emergency brake engaged (by accident) and hardly noticed it? That's because most emergency brakes on automobiles engage the rear brakes only.

HERE'S THE SIMPLE TRUTH. IF YOU ONLY USE YOUR REAR BRAKE, IT'S GOING TO TAKE YOU LONGER TO STOP THAN ME DURING AN EMERGENCY STOP. EVERY–SINGLE–TIME.

Cruiser Magazine said it best:

> *"Hopefully, deliberate avoidance of the front brake [only using the rear brake] is limited to a few dinosaurs (who are likely to be extinct rather quickly). The don't-use-the-front-brake concept shares one thing with all those other [misguided] braking theories: it's wrong."*[1]

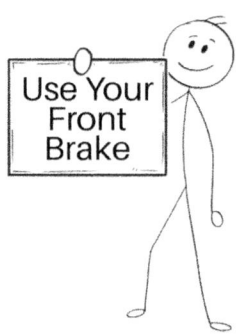

SIXTEEN

Seek Approval

Someone once said this to me.

"My wife will never agree to me getting a motorcycle, so I'm going to buy one anyway. After all, she didn't ask me before she bought new furniture."

That might be true, but furniture is different than a motorcycle.

If you buy a motorcycle without checking with your spouse, you're asking for trouble. Choosing to ride is a big deal.

For some, the conversation will be short and sweet. For others, it will be like throwing water on hot grease.

When I told my wife I wanted a motorcycle, she wasn't thrilled.

Instead of reacting, I stayed calm and told her *why* I wanted one. I promised her I would take ownership of my safety and do everything I could to reduce my risks. Then I listened to her concerns.

I didn't know at the time that I would end up writing a series of books on motorcycles. That might have helped me convince her.

After I showed her where my life insurance papers were (her idea), she gave me her blessing, and I started looking.

It's also important to have people around to help guide you.

Spouses and close friends know your strengths and weaknesses. Are you accident-prone? Do you make impulsive and careless purchases?

They know and can point this out.

Besides the obvious risks associated with crashing, there are also financial considerations.

Owning a motorcycle costs money—even if it just sits in your garage.

It's like having a horse. I know. I have both.

Actually, my wife claims the horse.

And where are you going to keep your bike? If it's in your one-car garage and your wife parks her car in there now, *she will care.*

So will your husband if things are reversed.

And don't overlook the fact that motorcycles also take time. You'll likely want to ride when your spouse wants to spend the day together.

And who's going to watch the kids when you do ride?

There's probably some truth in the old saying, "It's better to ask for forgiveness than permission." But not in this case.

ANYWAY YOU LOOK AT IT, RIDING A MOTORCYCLE IMPACTS THOSE AROUND YOU.

That's why it's best to seek their approval—first.

SEVENTEEN

Learn How to Drive a Manual First

I think fewer folks take up riding motorcycles nowadays because fewer people know how to drive a car with a manual transmission.

But that's just a theory.

This might sound silly, but one of the most difficult skills to master on a motorcycle is the mechanics of shifting. If you can operate a car with a manual, you'll catch on quicker because you already understand how to use the friction zone and shift through the gears.

I can only imagine how difficult it must be to learn how to operate a motorcycle for someone who's never driven a manual.

I would have struggled.

So, before you learn how to ride a motorcycle, why not learn how to operate a car with a manual transmission first?

Unfortunately, it might be hard to find one. Many car companies stopped making cars with manuals for the U.S. market years ago.

One idea is to find a friend with an older Honda that has a manual and ask them if they would be willing to teach you. I kept an Accord that had a manual far longer than I needed it so I could teach my kids how to drive it. I'm glad they both know how.

When someone asks me how difficult it is to ride a motorcycle, I always respond with this question:

"Can you drive a car with a manual transmission?"

If you can say yes, you'll have an
easier time learning than someone who can't.

EIGHTEEN

Ride a Scooter First

There's absolutely nothing wrong with riding a scooter.

Two wheels. Wind in my face. Riding in the cold, hot, and rain—all with the simplicity of an automatic transmission.

What's not to like about that?

I just looked up zero to sixty times for several 650cc scooters and, let's just say, if I was on a cruiser, I wouldn't challenge one.

Also, I found a segment called sport scooters that I wasn't familiar with. Hum. They look fun to me—especially since my current motorcycle seems to be getting heavier as I get older.

My first motorized two-wheel thing was a moped.

And that moped was the most enjoyable "thing" I've ever owned.

NINETEEN

Consider Another Craft

I like to try to convince wannabe riders NOT to ride a motorcycle and instead choose a different craft. It's how I sleep so well at night.

That's what my parents did when I was twelve. They were right.

After all, I managed to stay away from them for the first forty years of my life—as long as you don't count my Honda Express moped.

Since this is my book, I'm going to tell you what I really think. I don't think everyone is cut out to ride a motorcycle!

Are you a hothead, a pothead, or someone who jumps into things before thinking them through?

Maybe getting into motorcycles isn't such a good idea.

Are you accident-prone? Do you make bad decisions in other areas of your life? Are your friends suggesting you try something different?

Maybe your friends are right.

Do you have credit card debt or trouble paying your bills?

Maybe you should get your finances in order first.

The best advice in this book might be for you to consider NOT riding a motorcycle.

My parents wouldn't let me get a motorcycle when I was a kid.

I patiently waited until it was the right time for me—at forty.

If people who read my books ended up choosing a different craft other than riding, that would make me happy—weird, I know.

You don't have to ride a motorcycle
to have a complete life.

TWENTY

Keep Your Eyes Level in a Curve

Recall earlier when I described my first ride with Fred?

Right after I responded to Fred's email that the pace of our ride on the way back was toward the top end of my comfort zone, he replied, *"Are you keeping your eyes level with the ground in curves?"*

Hum, what's he talking about?

He sent a link to an article that described it.

I googled it, and sure enough, Fred was right—again.

I went out the next day, found some curves, and tried pivoting my head so my eyes (head) always stayed level with the horizon.

Wow! In an instant, curves became doable and fun! It sure helps to have a motorcycle mentor who knows what he's talking about.

See Figure 20-1 (below).

The crazy thing is that tilting your head even a few degrees from being horizontal with the ground makes your brain have to work extra hard to figure out clues of what's going on.

Keep your eyes level with the ground when you're in a curve. You'll notice the difference immediately.

Figure 20-1 Keep Your Eyes Level With the Horizon

As an example, try this.

The next time you're watching sports on television, tilt your head a little bit and notice how hard it is to follow what's going on.

With a small amount of tilt, your brain can still figure things out (even a football game). But as you tilt your head more and more, it becomes increasingly unclear what you're seeing.

A football game becomes difficult to follow.

The same thing holds true when you lean your bike over through a curve but keep your head in line with your motorcycle instead of tilting your head/neck so your eyes are horizontal with the ground.

Want to see what I'm talking about?

The next time you're in a car, tilt your head while going straight. See how that feels odd? Next, try tilting your head slightly when you're going around a curve. Tilting your head in a car while going around a curve would simulate *not* tilting your head on a motorcycle.

Once I started following Fred's advice, everything changed.

This motorcycle hack
was a game changer for me.

TWENTY-ONE

Rider Fear

Most riders experience what I call *rider fear*.

It's real, but for some reason, riders seem awkward talking about it.

I covered the topic in more detail (what is it, who has it, and how to overcome it) in *Motorcycle Smarts*.

Here, I'll just introduce it and make a bold recommendation.

Rider fear manifests itself in different ways—from an anxiety when you think about riding—to an all-out panic attack when you do.

If you've experienced it, you know exactly what I'm talking about.

The most important thing to know about rider fear is that it's your friend. It tells you what to do next. It must be respected.

It also needs to become less intense to signal you're on the right path. If it doesn't, you might want to consider a different craft.

Listen closely. Rider fear is one of our most precious gifts.

TWENTY-TWO

The Motorcycle Wave

If you've ridden for more than a mile, you've figured this out already.

The motorcycle wave is something to behold.

After my first Saturday morning ride, I emailed Fred to inquire. *"Yes. It's the motorcycle wave. I've been waving to riders my entire life."*

Sometimes it means "Hello," and other times it means something a little bit deeper. On the first warm Saturday in spring, it almost always means, "Wow, I forgot how amazing this is."

Several years back, I did an entire *Motorcycle Mentor Podcast* on the topic of the motorcycle wave.

Just throw out your left hand and wave however it feels natural.

I'm embarrassed to say this, but for a period of time early in my journey, I didn't wave to everyone. I felt comfortable waving to riders on similar bikes. But when I met someone on a different style of bike, I waited for them to wave to me first.

One day, I decided that was silly. I now wave to *all* riders.

And when riders don't wave back, It's on them.

TWENTY-THREE

Riding in the Rain

I chuckle every time I hear someone say:

"My motorcycle has never seen rain."

I don't understand why this is something to brag about.

When you make this statement, what you're really saying is that you don't ride much. That's fine, but I'm not sure why it wouldn't be just as easy to say this instead.

"I have a motorcycle, but I don't ride it very much."

If you ride for long enough, you'll get wet. It's guaranteed.

I've been caught in wet weather when the weatherperson said there was no chance of rain. I've had to suit up when it was pouring because I needed to make it to the next city before it got dark.

I've been caught in fog, wet, cold, and heat—and even a popup thunderstorm from hell in Idaho.

You can read all about that in *Motorcycle Dream Ride.*

If your bike has never seen the rain, you certainly haven't ventured far from home or done much touring—and you've also missed out on one of the most joyous things you can do on two wheels.

More on that later.

TWENTY-FOUR

Don't Ride for the Wrong Reasons

Why do you want to ride a motorcycle?

I'm asking because I believe that some ride for the wrong reasons. How do I know? I get emails all the time from them.

Some ride to get back at their spouse (friends or parents).

At least one rider wants to ride because their friend was killed on a motorcycle. I was shocked when I read her email.

> *"A very close high school friend of mine was just killed by a drunk driver on her motorcycle. Instead of shying away from riding, this has made me want to ride even more. My question is this. She was built like me, 5 feet tall and 95 pounds. She was riding a 2009 Ducati Monster when she died. I do not know what size bike would work for someone of my stature. I have been reading website after website with no luck. Can someone please help?"*
> —*Jane*

I think we can all agree the scenario above strikes a deeper emotion than most folks (including me) are trained to analyze.

All I can say is please
don't buy a motorcycle to
get back at a loved one
or because your friend
died riding one.

And the email I get most often goes something like this:
"My husband wants me to ride my own bike, but I don't want to."

Peer pressure makes me sick.

TWENTY-FIVE

Assume They Will Exit

If you're riding on an interstate, assume the motorist on your left is going to take the exit on your right—across the lane in front of you.

The bulletproof way to do this is to avoid being in their path.

The next best way to do this is to avoid being in their blind spot—the position to their side and toward the back of their car. If this isn't possible, pull up to a position up front so they can easily see you.

The first time this happened to me was on my very first ride on an interstate a week or so after I purchased my first motorcycle.

I'd be dead several times over if I hadn't done this throughout my riding journey. Just last week, I was in my car, and the driver on my left turned so hard and crossed in front of me to catch the exit on my right that I thought he might lose control and crash.

I had just repositioned myself to be out of his path.

With practice, this mindset to avoid the spaces a distracted driver might want to go to will become a part of your normal psyche.

TWENTY-SIX

Use Your Front Brake—Please!

Looking at the crash data trends, it's clear that many riders still don't believe that using their front brake is the right thing to do. If this book convinces one rider, I've done what I set out to do.

Harry Hurt, famous for the Hurt Report, said:

"I still do consulting for police departments and have investigated a number of police motorcycle accidents over the years. Police motor officers get some extensive training. I mean really good training. But even professionals make the same sort of mistakes as novices, and today's riders seem to have the same sort of accidents as those in the NHTSA [Hurt] Report."[1]

Hurt continued ...

"For example, an L.A.P.D officer on a police Kawasaki had a pickup truck back out in front of him. We measured a perfectly straight rear-only tire skid 200 feet long right into the side of the pickup. The length of the skid gives us a pretty good idea of his speed, something like 60 mph. But even at that speed, he could have stopped short of a collision if he had just used the front brake. It's the same mistake riders were making in the 1970s."

USING YOUR FRONT BRAKE IS SIMPLE. CONVINCING RIDERS THAT IT'S THE RIGHT THING TO DO HAS PROVEN TO BE DIFFICULT OVER TIME.

From all my research, I believe Hurt was right when he said that riders are making the same mistakes we did forty years ago.

Riders are still crashing because they aren't using their front brake, don't understand what happens when they lock up their rear tire, and because they don't know what to do when going wide in a turn.

More on that later.

Yes, I'm starting to repeat myself about using your front brake in hopes of busting the myth. If you're a front brake user already, please bear with me. But the crash data suggests that I have <u>more</u> than a handful of riders still left to convince.

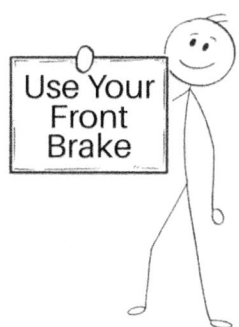

TWENTY-SEVEN

Practice the Correct Way

Let's take a look at what Hurt said in the last chapter about the highly trained officer skidding his motorcycle into the side of a truck because he only used his rear brake.

To Harry's point, how can it be that someone with so much skills training instinctively grabbed their rear brake in a pinch?

It's because what we do during normal rides is what we're going to do when we're about to crash. It's called *muscle memory*.

I cover muscle memory in more depth in *Motorcycle Smarts*.

My motorcycle mentor Fred insisted that I use my front brake even when putzing around in my neighborhood—because that's what I would do in a panic situation.

He was right.

TWENTY-EIGHT

Countersteering in Curves

The crash studies are clear. Curves are tough on motorcyclists.

According to a Florida Department of Transportation Report, 57 percent of fatal single-vehicle motorcycle crashes occurred in curves.[1]

The part of this that people don't want to talk about is that when riders crash in curves, it's usually their fault—good ole rider error.

Sure, there could be debris on the pavement or an animal jumped out, but that's rare. *Most single-vehicle crashes are due to rider error.*

Countersteering isn't just how you control your motorcycle under normal conditions. It's what you use to keep from crashing in a curve.

Let's look at a common single-vehicle crash scenario.

Let's say you're going around a sweeping curve to the left, have misjudged your speed, and you're going wide. See Figure 28-1 (below).

In this situation, you need to act quickly:

1. Look where you want to go deep in the curve,
2. Push on the inside handlebar to tighten your turn, and
3. Trust your tires to carry you through.

Believe me. This might not feel natural, but you do it anyway.

The first time I did this to tighten a turn I had misjudged and was going wide in, I felt disoriented. I was certain my tires would lose traction, but they didn't—even though I asked them to do a lot.

I safely exited the turn and silently thanked my motorcycle mentor for teaching me to use countersteering and trust my tires in a pinch.

Figure 28-1 Countersteering to Tighten Turn
(Push on Left Handlebar)

Now you know why I'm so adamant that all riders
UNDERSTAND COUNTERSTEERING with their HEAD.

I've seen hundreds of videos on Youtube where the rider goes wide in a turn, runs off the side of the road, and crashes.

I can't help but wonder how many of these single-vehicle accidents could have been avoided if the rider had used countersteering and trusted his tires to tighten the turn.

Head knowledge rocks.

TWENTY-NINE

Riding in Groups

Honestly, I'm not a huge fan of riding in groups. Neither was Fred.

This chapter in draft form was much longer. But I decided that I wasn't going to change anyone's mind, so I whittled it down.

At the end of the day, you get to decide whether you want to ride in a group. Instead of trying to talk you out of it, I'm simply going to highlight a few things for you to think about when you do.

Before I proceed, I recognize that riding with others can be one of the best parts of motorcycling. What I'm mostly suggesting here is that riding in a group should be done with some forethought.

It's when you ride with a group of riders with varying skill levels on different types of motorcycles that it gets more complicated.

Riding with one buddy is very different than riding with ten.

Some bikes have smaller fuel tanks that require more frequent fill-ups. Some bikes like to roll down the Interstate at higher speeds. Some bikes will have to work harder to go much over Interstate speed limits.

Some riders like to knock out 200 miles between stops.

Other riders might prefer to stop more often.

Some riders prefer a staggered formation. Others don't.

 Riding in a group takes more planning and execution to do it SAFELY.

Understanding this is a great place to start.

What are you going to do if riders get stopped at a traffic light?

Does everyone have clarity on the next designated stop?

Are you going to ride in a staggered formation or as individuals?

What are you going to do if Bobby goes missing?

Do you have a contact person you can notify if Bobby crashes?

These are just some of the things that go through my mind when I ride in a group. And sometimes, that feels exhausting.

Now you know why I like riding
by myself or with just Mike.

THIRTY

Ride If You Want to Improve

If you want to become a better rider, you have to ride.

There's no substitute, no shortcut, no book you can read—that will magically make you better.

Mental preparation and book smarts are great catalysts, but you have to put your butt in a motorcycle seat if you want to get better.

The late Larry Grodsky, Stayin' Safe instructor and columnist, used to say that you had to ride over a certain number of miles every year to maintain your riding skills. Larry was probably right.

But it also matters how frequently you ride.

In other words, it's not the number of miles you ride each month. It's the number of *times* you ride that will determine your progress.

My mentor Fred wanted me to ride as often as I could when I first started—even if it was for only a few miles in my neighborhood.

He used to tell me:

"FREQUENT SHORTER RIDES ARE BETTER THAN INFREQUENT LONGER RIDES."

If you only ride a couple of times a year, don't think we can't spot you. You're the rider who puts both feet down way too early at stops, looks unstable in low-speed turns, and duck-walks his bike with pride.

We see you out in droves on the first warm Saturday of spring.

And yes, you look amazing all decked out.

Just realize you're not fooling anyone except yourself—and maybe your friends who ride twice a year along with you.

NOTE: I realize that for every mile you ride, you're at risk of crashing. Therefore, it's possible you're less likely to crash if you ride twice a year (with poor skills) than you are if you ride 9,000 miles a year (proficiently). This is just something I wanted to point out because it goes against what Larry and I are suggesting.

THIRTY-ONE

Holding on a Hill

When you're stopped on an uphill or downhill slope, you'll need to hold one of your brakes to keep the bike from rolling.

Most seem to think that using your rear brake is easier.

But, the truth is you need to be able to use either.

A couple of blocks from my house, there's a stop sign at the end of a pretty significant hill. The problem here is that the road also slopes to the left so severely that I can't reach the ground with my left foot.

In other words, since I have to use my right foot to steady my bike, I have to use my front brake to keep the bike from rolling back.

With a little practice, holding the front brake while navigating the throttle and clutch (and launching the bike) will be a piece of cake.

Practice accordingly.

THIRTY-TWO

Tight Formations

I've never been a fan of tight formations, and neither was Fred.

And why would *anyone* ride side-by-side?

This seems especially foolish on open roads like interstates.

The only valid argument for riding in a tight formation *might* be in situations where more riders can get through traffic signals.

But I still think it's risky.

In any case, my mentor Fred thought it was best to ride far enough apart that you could avoid hitting the guy in front of you if they made an emergency stop or crashed.

In other words, ride like they were in an automobile, and you don't know them. Isn't there a three-second rule on that?

I've told Mike more than once when I was leading:

> *"I'm not even thinking about you behind me.*
> *If you crash into me, though, I'm going to be ticked."*

THIRTY-THREE

Leave Your Husband at Home

Riding with a passenger on the back of a motorcycle requires a unique set of riding skills. It's not easy. It can be dangerous. I still don't do it.

For this reason, it's probably a good idea for beginning riders not to carry friends, or spouses, or homeless people they just met.

You'll be ready after your skills improve.

If your spouse wants to participate, tell him you're not comfortable carrying passengers and that you think it's too risky right now.

Ask him to meet you at the destination in a car.

Your kids need at least one parent—so my wife tells me.

RIDING A MOTORCYCLE SOLO IS CHALLENGING. RIDING A MOTORCYCLE WITH SOMEONE IN THE SEAT BEHIND YOU IS EVEN more CHALLENGING.

Not so fast here—baby steps rule.

THIRTY-FOUR

Riding in Groups: The Psychology

The thing that bothers me most about riding in a group is there's pressure for riders to ride more aggressively than they normally would.

Every rider feels pressure to stay with the rider ahead of them. And the most aggressive riders are the ones who tend to be out front.

Fred warned me about this. He called it the *psychology of riding*.

Honestly, I'm not as proficient when I'm in a group. I'm distracted. I focus on the wrong things. I feel pressure to keep up. I feel like the rider behind me is grading my riding skills.

"I thought Dave wrote books on motorcycles. You'd never know it by looking at the way he just took that corner."

A beta reader for this book wrote this in his notes back to me.

I thought they were worth including here.

"David, the psychology of trying to keep up with riders ahead can positively kill in group rides. I've seen it happen first-hand. Riders should never try to keep up. I would re-emphasize and expand this life-saving measure. Avoid group rides, especially with strangers. Bad things are much more likely to happen in group rides."

Thanks Mark. Great advice.

THIRTY-FIVE

Look Where You Want to Go

There's a concept that all riders need to understand.

Your motorcycle goes where you're looking.

The takeaway here is that you need to look where you want to go. It's kind of freaky how this works, but it does. I've tested it.

This head knowledge is important because the last thing you want to do when you're trying to dodge something is to look at it.

Why? Because that's exactly where you're going to go.

This will take some mental discipline, I know.

So, when you see a hazard you want to avoid—an object in the road, a car coming at you—don't look at it. Instead, pick a spot in the road that misses it and focus on that.

This sounds so simple, yet it can be so hard. If an animal runs in front of you, your natural instinct will be to look at it. But don't!

LOOK WHERE YOU WANT TO GO
BECAUSE THAT'S WHERE YOU'RE GOING.

This is one reason rider coaches tell us to look deep into a curve. Our motorcycle goes where our eyes tell it to. See Figure 35-1 (below).

So, be careful where you look!

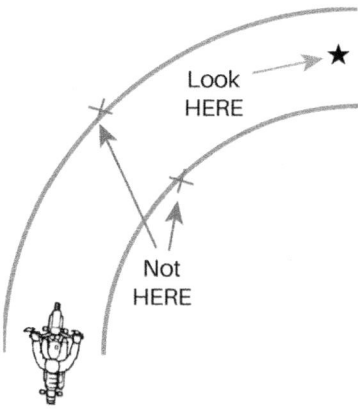

Figure 35-1 Look Deep Into Curve

NOTE: Target fixation is the term used to describe when a rider focuses on the thing they don't want to hit— the place they don't want to go.

THIRTY-SIX

The Physics of Hills

When you're going uphill, physics says you have more traction.

There's also added stability because your suspension is loaded.

When you're going downhill, physics says you have less traction—and because your suspension is unloaded, you have less stability.

This might not matter so much if you're going in a straight line. But when you're leaned over in a curve, it could make a difference.

The worst is when the curve is at the top of a hill, and the road is starting to crest to a downhill stretch.

When I'm riding roads with switchbacks, I'm always more cautious when the curve is going downhill or cresting at the top.

Riding up the mountain to Pikes Peak was much more enjoyable than riding back down because I knew physics was on my side.

Going around a curve at the top of a hill is a hot spot for something bad because the rate of change in the slope is the real driver.

You might have noticed road signs on interstates warning trucks to slow down when there's a curve cresting the top of a hill because of the potential tipping hazard. Physics is the same on a motorcycle.

THIRTY-SEVEN

Over the Shoulder Every Time

I'm not going to sugarcoat it. Motorcycle mirrors suck.

Sure, some are better than others, but I'm convinced there's never a good reason NOT to look over your shoulder when you change lanes.

The risks of getting it wrong are too great—but I think you know that already.

While we're talking about motorcycle mirrors, I'd love to suggest something that oftentimes makes them more usable.

They're called *mirror extenders*. On some bikes, they're a must.

It's usually a piece of material that attaches between your current mount and the mirror that puts them higher or farther out so you can see better. Just google mirror extenders for your make and model.

Like eyes in the back of your head.

THIRTY-EIGHT

How to Drop Your Motorcycle?

This might be the easiest thing you ever do on a bike. Honestly, there are so many good ways to drop a motorcycle. I'll mention a few.

Let's talk about zero-speed drops. Anything faster is a crash.

About half of these drops involve a *problem with the side stand.*

1. You think it's down, but it's not.
2. You think it's on solid ground, but it's not.
3. You think it's fully extended, but it's not.
4. You think it's in gear, but it's not and rolls off the stand.
5. You're in the process of extending it, but something trips you up—a caught shoestring on a foot peg, perhaps.

The other half of these drops involve *poor footing.*

1. Your foot gets caught as you're putting it down.
2. Your foot slips on gravel, loose ground, or something slippery (like oil or antifreeze).
3. Your foot doesn't reach the ground like you anticipated because you're on a slope or uneven ground.

And just so you know, it's almost a certainty that you'll have lots of folks watching when it happens.

One more thing. If you're trying to look cool to impress someone when conditions are poor, you might as well count on dropping it.

———

Because that's usually when it happens.

THIRTY-NINE

Riding Makes You a Better Driver

I'm convinced that one of the best things about learning how to ride a motorcycle well is that it makes us better drivers.

Maybe it's because we learn how to spot danger more quickly, or because we realize how vulnerable we really are. Maybe it's because we begin to anticipate the movement of others like we have superpowers.

My driving didn't improve immediately, but it did over time. It took months for me to realize that I was starting to drive like I rode.

I looked for drivers to do the unexpected.

I noticed cars making left turns in front of me.

I always left margin for what-ifs.

The head knowledge part of riding a motorcycle translates perfectly to driving a car. Sometimes it feels like I have a sixth sense that I never had before.

Whether you continue to ride or not, the skills you develop will make you a better driver for the rest of your life.

And that's a pretty powerful thing.

FORTY

Avoid Riding at Night

Every motorcycle crash study I've seen says the same thing.

Riding a motorcycle at night is riskier.

I don't think that's hard to imagine.

Anytime Mike and I are on a two-wheeled adventure, we always try to avoid riding at night. This usually means we start each day early.

While our record isn't perfect (long days happen), we've never been caught riding at night because we were lazy getting up.

The closest call we've had, so close I really don't even like reliving it, happened when Mike and I were riding at night in Virginia.

Before we checked in to our hotel for the evening, we stopped at a burger spot for dinner. On our short ride to the hotel, Mike didn't see a pickup truck coming and started to pull out into the intersection.

I shouted in my helmet, "STOP, Mike STOP!"

He rolled off the throttle, grabbed the clutch and brake, and came to an awkward stop a bike-length into the intersection.

The truck flew past doing at least twice the speed limit.

The occupants looked like they were having a party on four wheels.

My heart raced. It was a close call. We both knew it.

For the rest of that evening (and many times since), I've thought about how our lives could have changed in that instant.

We both would have easily seen the truck in the light of day—and the driver would have easily seen us. We usually think the main risk of riding at night is that others can't see us.

That evening nearly ended in tragedy because we didn't see them.

It is true that riding at night isn't an automatic death sentence. But neither is riding after you've had four beers or an argument with your wife. That's not what I'm suggesting.

I'm saying that your chances of crashing are higher if you do *any* of the above. What you choose to do with that truth is up to you.

Want to decrease your chances of crashing? Don't ride at night.

And there's also the increased risk of hitting animals.

Larry Grodsky, the owner of Stayin' Safe motorcycle training, died in 2006 while riding at night when he collided with a deer. Larry was an amazing rider and writer.

Weeks before he crashed, he told his girlfriend, Maryann Puglisi.

"That's how I'm going to go. It's going to be a deer."

Puglisi told reporters, "He could deal with all the idiot drivers, but at night when a deer jumps in your path, that's it, and he knew it."[1]

I didn't know Larry, but one of my mentors, Pete Tamblyn, knew him well and worked as an instructor at Stayin' Safe.

Larry's articles in *Rider* magazine were whimsical and blunt.

His death was a reminder of just how fragile life can be—and that there are risks of riding at night that can't be overcome even with the highest level of riding skills.

FORTY-ONE

How to Ride at Night

I know this sounds confusing.

In the last chapter, I told you to avoid riding at night.

Now, I'm giving you tips on how to do it.

If you're a fair-weather rider who reserves his motorcycle for sunny afternoon strolls, you can probably avoid riding at night altogether.

If you're someone who likes to ride to far-away places, you'll likely get caught riding at night—at least once in a while.

Here are some tips when you do.

First and foremost, assume motorists don't see you. The fact is they won't be able to very easily when it's dark. The best solution for this is to wear bright gear that has reflective pieces.

It's also a good idea to add aftermarket running lights up front.

Mike has some, and it's amazing how big a difference they make.

It's also prudent to leave extra margin, ride less aggressively, and find a comfortable place in traffic and stay there.

As I mentioned in the last chapter, riding at night also brings out an entirely new set of hazards—wildlife.

There's only so much you can do here.

Anytime Mike and I get caught riding at night in rural areas, we always try to find a car or two to follow behind. We tell ourselves that the cars will scare off curious critters before we get there.

I'm not sure that's true, but it makes us feel proactive.

When I first started riding, I took my Honda VFR for an evening ride. It was early spring and there was hardly any traffic.

The air was crisp and cool. I could feel the temperature differences at the bottom and tops of hills. I could smell the fragrances of spring.

It felt absolutely magical.

For some reason, I decided to hop on an Interstate nearby. Once I came up to speed, I lowered my chest down onto my tank bag.

I'll never forget the peace of that moment.

The noise of the wind onto my body silenced as I moved into the protection of my shield and faring. It felt like I was all alone in the still of darkness. I hadn't yet made the connection that what I was doing was risker—and I liked it that way.

I'm not a *never-ride-at-night guy.* I'm an *avoid-riding-at-night guy* who believes my chances of crashing are higher when I do.

THE BOTTOM LINE FOR ME IS THAT I ONLY RIDE AT NIGHT WHEN THERE'S A GOOD ENOUGH REASON TO.

And that could be as silly as wanting to experience an evening with Mother Nature.

FORTY-TWO

Practice Lifting Your Bike

There's probably some truth to the idea that it's only a matter of time before your bike ends up lying on the ground. It can happen so fast.

I'm not talking about a crash. I'm talking about a zero-speed drop.

If you don't count the mishap in my garage that I wrote about earlier, my first drop took years to complete. I'll share that story soon. My second drop occurred a decade after that in Utah.

I shared the details of that drop in *Motorcycle Dream Ride.*

In this chapter, I'm not going to give you the steps to lifting your particular motorcycle because an online video would be worth a thousand words. Instead, I'm simply going to encourage you to learn the steps (head knowledge) and then see if you can do it.

Most of the time, even a smallish person can lift a biggish bike, but that's not always the case. If you discover you can't lift her by yourself, you'll know to look for help when it happens.

All valuable information.

FORTY-THREE

Wear Bright Gear

The only folks on motorcycles I've almost hit while driving a car were wearing dull-colored riding gear.

Obviously, I'm not suggesting this is scientific, but I am making a point that folks can't see you so well if your gear isn't very bright. And what's up with camouflage-colored stuff a few of you are wearing?

That's about as stupid as stupid gets.

Hurt found that motorists' failure to recognize and detect motorcycles was the leading cause of accidents.[1]

Reading this changed the way I ride. Now, I assume motorists have a hard time seeing me and judging my speed and distance.

It's your responsibility to be seen.

Have you ever pulled out in front of a motorcycle when you were in a car? I have many times, not because I have a thing against motorcycles, but because I didn't see them or misjudged their speed.

I'm betting you have too.

I almost hit a dude on a motorcycle the other day because I didn't see him. He blended in perfectly with his hunting gear.

Is that the look he was after?

Want to lower your
chances of crashing?
Wear bright-colored
gear—and add some
running lights.

There's a reason folks doing road work wear hi-vis yellow shirts.

So motorists will see them.

Part Three: Crash Avoidance Hacks

In my book, *Motorcycle Smarts*, I spent a great deal of time explaining lowside and highside crashes my way.

What are they? What triggers them? How can you avoid them?

These crashes are critical to understand because they're avoidable in most situations. I'll get to that shortly.

The topic of *lowside* and *highside* crashes is one of the most under-discussed topics in motorcycling. Even the most popular motorcycle skills books hardly mention them—maybe a sentence or two.

It's not an easy topic to explain, but they're critical to understand. So important, in fact, that I promised myself I would explain them in every skills book on motorcycles I write.

In this section, I'll cover the basics—which is still more than *any* other book on motorcycling you'll find. Consider this a bonus section.

You can find more in *Motorcycle Smarts*.

FORTY-FOUR

Running up on a Crash

Mike and I were riding back from a friend's lake house (tough life) when we saw the man standing on the side of the road.

As we rode by, we could see his mangled Harley in the ditch.

He looked dazed and in shock.

We cautiously turned around and went back to help.

When we made it to the scene, the man was talking on his phone. Mike asked if he was okay, and the gentleman moved the phone away from his mouth.

"I think so. I'm banged up, and my shoulder hurts."

A few seconds later, he pulled the phone away again.

"Where are we?"

If you've read *Motorcycle Dream Ride*, you know that Mike is the navigator on the team. I turned to him and waited for his response.

"We're on Hwy 278, four miles west of the Subway in Addison."

The man tried to repeat Mike's description, but he couldn't get the words in the right order. In frustration, he handed the phone to Mike and asked him to describe where we were.

The rider was scraped up and holding his left shoulder. He was in a lot of pain. I knew it was going to get worse before it got better.

My mom taught me that when I was a kid.

Just having us there seemed to make him feel better. He was obviously grateful that we had stopped.

His Harley was a mangled mess. The back trunk had popped open, and stuff was scattered everywhere. Mike and I gathered everything we could find and placed it in a pile next to his bike.

A few minutes later, a Sheriff in an unmarked car pulled up. I felt relieved—relieved he found us with Mike's directions, and relieved we no longer needed to be in charge.

We stayed around for a few more minutes, asked again if there was anything we could do (they said no), and then left.

On our ride back, I tried to figure out what had happened.

An Analysis of the Crash

I sometimes wonder if I should have applied to work for the National Transportation Safety Board (NTSB) studying why airplanes crash.

All that to say, I like trying to figure out *what happened*.

To begin with, the rider crashed alone in a single-vehicle accident. He didn't say anything about a deer running out in front of him, or a motorist forcing him off the road, or a mechanical failure of any kind.

The road was in good shape with no potholes or slick spots.

And just in case you've watched too many movies depicting the deep south as bush-league—*the road was paved.*

My best guess is he misjudged the curve, started going wide, and didn't know what to do to correct it. From there, he likely lowsided.

Had he used countersteering to tighten his radius, he could have stopped for a soda at the Subway four miles down the road (on the right) in Addison, Alabama. Instead, he was standing on the side of the road in the middle of nowhere with a busted bike and shoulder.

THIS ACCIDENT SHOULDN'T HAVE HAPPENED. THE RIDER CRASHED ALONE ON A DRY, SUNNY DAY WITH NO OBSTACLES OTHER THAN A SIMPLE CURVE.

And there was no one around
to blame but himself.

FORTY-FIVE

Lowside and Highside Crashes

In the next several chapters, I'm going to explain lowside and highside crashes: what causes them and how you can avoid them.

The illustrations are from real crashes captured on video.

Most riders have probably heard of lowside and highside crashes. But I'm going to dial it up a notch and explain how you can virtually eliminate them. Talk about reducing your chances of crashing!

The concepts of lowside and highside crashes aren't that difficult to understand as long as you don't get bogged down with the physics of how these crashes happen.

Power through with me.

Reducing these crashes changes the crash data!

Quickie Definitions

Before we get started, here's an introductory definition for each.

In a nutshell, a *lowside* crash is when your motorcycle slides on its side, and you slide on the ground behind it. A *highside* crash is when your bike tosses you up and over the handlebars.

I'll explain both in more detail a little later.

Just in case I lose you in the details, I want to tell you up-front the most important thing you need to know.

On a motorcycle, BAD THINGS HAPPEN when you lock up (skid) your tires— especially your REAR tire.

I feel better knowing I got that point out there!
It's so important that I'll say it again.

LOCKING UP YOUR REAR TIRE IS BAD!

The topic of lowside and highside crashes is well understood by rider coaches and authors of motorcycle skills books. Yet, most riders don't understand what triggers them.[1] If this is true, our current motorcycle training programs need to be modified.

Here's one man's attempt to thoroughly explain lowside and highside crashes in simple-to-understand language. If you understand and implement the recommendations in this section, you WILL slash your chances of crashing.

FORTY-SIX

Why Understanding LS and HS Crashes Matters

Why is understanding these crashes so important?

In a nutshell, many lowside and highside crashes are rider-induced single-vehicle crashes. Let's take a look at some of the data.

The Hurt Report found that roughly 25 percent of all motorcycle accidents were single-vehicle crashes *(bike did not hit another vehicle)*, and 75 percent were multi-vehicle crashes *(bike did hit another vehicle)*.

The Hurt Report also found that rider error accounted for approximately 67 percent of single-vehicle crashes and 33 percent of multi-vehicle crashes. When you do the math:

(.67 x 25) = 17% of all motorcycle crashes
were single-vehicle crashes caused by rider error

AND ...

(.33 x 75) = 25% of all motorcycle crashes
were multi-vehicle crashes caused by rider error.

YIELDS ...

*(17% + 25%) = 42% of all motorcycle crashes
were caused by rider error!*

That's right. Nearly half (42 percent) of all the motorcycle crashes Hurt studied were caused by rider error!

And Hurt isn't the only one to make these conclusions.

Other crash studies done more recently show similar results.

Understanding lowside and highside crashes is important because these are oftentimes rider-induced single-vehicle crashes.

To all the riders who say, "I can't change my chances of crashing," I say nonsense. You CAN reduce your risks of being in an accident by improving your offensive and defensive riding skills.

Next, let's dive into lowside crashes.

FORTY-SEVEN

Lowside Crashes

A lowside crash is easier to understand than a highside crash, so let's tackle that one first.

What Is a Lowside?

A lowside crash is when your motorcycle loses stability control, falls on its side sliding, and dumps you (the rider) on the ground behind it. Some refer to a lowside as a "slide-out" because that's sort of what happens—your rear end slides out.

Figure 47-1 (below) shows a rider who has just lowsided.

Figure 47-1 Lowside Crash
(Motorcycle Slides Out and Dumps Rider)

A lowside occurs when your rear tire (more likely) or front tire (less likely) loses traction with the asphalt. This can happen when you lock up (skid) a tire using your brakes or accelerate too hard in a curve.

NOTE: A skidding tire (which has kinetic friction) has less grip than a rolling tire (which has static friction).

What Triggers Most Lowsides?

Lowside Trigger #1
Rear tire locks up (skids) due to over-braking while in a curve.

If you lock up your rear tire when you're going around a curve, you'll most likely lowside. When your bike is leaning over, it needs the rotational control and friction between the rear tire and the pavement to keep the bike upright.

See Figure 47-2 (below).

Figure 47-2 Beginning of a Lowside (Rear Tire Locks
Up Due to Over-Braking While in a Curve)

Once you lose static friction (by locking the rear tire), the back tire will slide out, and the bike will fall on its side—dumping you on the ground behind it.

Lowside Trigger #2
Rear tire locks up (skids) due to over-braking while going straight.

If you lock up your rear tire when you're going in a straight line, you may or may not lowside. It depends on whether the skidding back tire slides around to the side. If the back tire slides around, you'll most likely lowside. If the skidding back tire stays in line with the front tire, you won't lowside.

If you lock up the rear tire when your front brake is applied (likely the case during an emergency stop), or when you're on a road that isn't perfectly flat, the skidding back tire will tend to come around to the side, and you'll most likely lowside.

Lowside Trigger #3
Rear tire spins due to over-accelerating while in a curve.

If you spin your rear tire when you're accelerating hard in a curve (bike is leaned over), you'll most likely lowside because a slipping tire has less friction than a tire in rotational contact with the pavement. Once the rear tire starts slipping, the back end will slide out, and you'll lowside.

Lowside Trigger #4
Front tire locks up (skids) due to over-braking while in a curve.

If you lock up your front tire when you're going around a curve, you'll most likely lowside. When your bike is leaning over, it needs the rotational control and friction between the front tire and the pavement to keep the bike upright.

See Figures 47-3 through 47-5 (below).

NOTE: In the particular example below, the rider wasn't going very fast since neither the rider nor bike slid very far. This isn't always the case. I'll break down a more typical lowside crash in the next chapter.

Figure 47-3 Beginning of a Low-Speed Lowside (Front Tire Locks Up Due to Over-Braking While in a Curve)

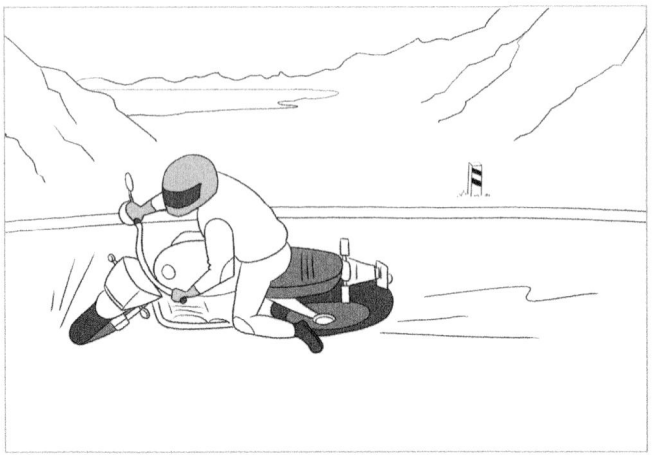

Figure 47-4 Middle of a Low-Speed Lowside (Front Tire Locks Up Due to Over-Braking While In a Curve)

Figure 47-5 End of a Low-Speed Lowside (Front Tire Locks Up Due to Over-Braking While in a Curve)

QUICK TIP: It's worth noting that locking up (skidding) your front tire when you're going in a relatively straight line (bike is upright) will NOT cause you to lowside. Tests have shown that a skidding front tire will continue in a straight line as long as the bike is in an upright position. One motorcycle myth debunked.

Locking up (skidding) your *front* tire requires a lot of lever force because weight is transferred to the front tire when you decelerate.

Locking up (skidding) your *rear* tire requires less lever force, especially if you're applying heavy front brake pressure at the same time.

This is why locking up your rear tire is the most likely TRIGGER for a lowside crash.

I've never lowsided, but I've spoken to several riders who have. They all said it happened really fast. In the blink of an eye, they went from *(everything is fine)* to *(my bike is sliding, and I'm sliding behind it)*.

If you think a lowside crash sounds painful, wait until I describe what happens in a highside crash.

UPDATE: I lowsided on a Backcountry Discovery Route in the George Washington National Forest in Virginia a few years later. The dirt road was a muddy mess. As my bike slid down a 10-foot embankment, I thought to myself. We'll never get it out of there. Two hours later, Mike and I manhandled it up the embankment—only because we didn't have another option. Right as we did, a group of riders came along, and two of the riders lowsided in the exact same spot I did. Luckily, I wasn't hurt, and neither were they.

Yes, it happened incredibly fast!

FORTY-EIGHT

Highside Crashes

Now that we understand lowside crashes and what causes them, let's look at highside crashes. I've spent hours going through slow-motion videos trying to understand the physics of a highside.

And this is what I've discovered.

I have to warn you. What you're about to learn is both *fascinating* and *terrifying*. The physics of a highside is fascinating! The thought of doing a highside is terrifying!

What Is a Highside?

A highside crash is when your motorcycle loses stability control and catapults you over the handlebars. You eventually hit the ground, often headfirst, and your bike tumbles toward you.

Figure 48-1 (below) shows a rider in the middle of a highside.

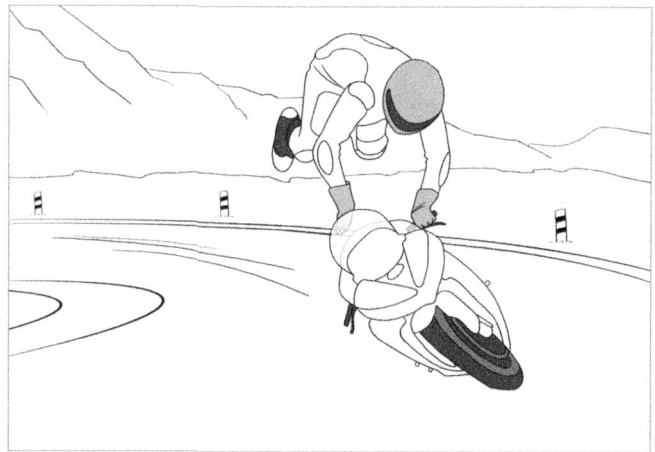

Figure 48-1 Highside Crash
(Motorcycle Catapults Rider)

Yeah, I know. Freaking scary, right?

A highside occurs when a skidding rear tire, which has slid out of alignment with the front tire, is released and allowed to rotate again.

Why It Happens

When the rear brake is released, the skidding rear tire (which has now slid out of alignment with the front) starts rotating again and immediately tracks inline behind the front tire. When this happens, the bike instantly sits up to a vertical position.

Since the motorcycle was leaned over (squatted) because the rear tire was sliding, the motion of the motorcycle snapping to a vertical position is like releasing a coiled-up spring.

This combination launches the rider into the air.

NOTE: I know this is a hard concept to understand. It's also a hard one to explain. I must be on my hundredth edit of this section. Stay with me. I have real examples (below and in the next chapter) that I think will help.

In Figure 48-2 (below) the skidding rear tire has moved out of alignment with the front. If the rider releases the rear brake and allows the tire to rotate again, he will most likely highside.

Figure 48-2 Rear Tire Slides Out

What Triggers Most Highsides?

Highside Trigger #1
Locking up rear tire (and then releasing it) while in a curve.

If you lock up (skid) your rear tire (by over-braking) while going around a curve, then release the rear brake and allow the tire to rotate again, you'll most likely highside.

> QUICK TIP: The faster you're going when you lock up your rear tire (and the farther out the skidding rear tire gets while it's locked up), the more abruptly the rear end will snap up once the rear tire is allowed to rotate again. If you're going slowly when you trigger a highside, it's unlikely that the highside snap will have enough energy to throw you off your bike.

Highside Trigger #2
Spinning rear tire (and then backing off throttle) while in a curve.

If you spin your rear tire (by over-accelerating) when going around a curve, then back off the throttle and allow the tire to regain traction, you'll most likely highside.

Highside Trigger #3
Locking up rear tire (and then releasing it) while on a straight road.

Unfortunately, you don't have to be in a curve to highside.

Let's assume you're making an emergency stop and applying both front and rear brakes. Since you're stopping so quickly, weight is transferred to the front of the bike.

Good, because it gives your front tire more stopping power.

Not so good, because it takes load off your rear tire (which makes it easier to lock up).

If you lock up your rear tire while you are braking hard with your front brake, the skidding back tire can skid around to the side because the front tire is braking hard, and the skidding rear tire lost directional control and static friction.

Now you're in trouble. If you then release the rear brake and allow the tire to rotate again, you'll most likely highside.

> NOTE: Here's the dilemma. Once your back tire starts skidding (over-braking), or spinning (over-accelerating), one of two things is likely to happen: You'll either *lowside* or *highside*.

I'm getting depressed thinking about my options.

While I have your attention, let me say it (again) because it's one of the most important points in this entire book.

Locking up your rear tire
is bad because it triggers
most lowside AND
highside crashes.

*If you understand this, you're on your way
to reducing your chances of crashing.
You're also way ahead of most riders.*

FORTY-NINE

Preventing Lowside and Highside Crashes

So far, we've established two things:

1. A skidding rear tire (over-braking, over-accelerating) is the trigger that causes most lowside and highside crashes.
2. Once your rear tire starts to skid, you don't have any good options to keep from crashing. See *Motorcycle Smarts*.

Now that we understand this (head knowledge), we need a way to keep from skidding our rear tire. It's as simple (and difficult) as that.

Well, there's the obvious: maintain your tires, ride with margin, slow down before the turn so you won't have to brake in the turn, and be easy on the throttle while you're in a turn.

But even better, there's something else you can do that will significantly reduce the chances of a lowside or highside crash.

RIDE A MOTORCYCLE EQUIPPED WITH AN ANTI- LOCK BRAKING SYSTEM (ABS).

ABS is an electronic system that prevents your tires from locking up. When the ABS detects that a tire is about to lock up, it automatically reduces brake pressure to that tire.

ABS has been standard on cars for years.

While ABS virtually eliminates most lowside and highside crashes due to over-braking, it doesn't keep you from spinning (over-accelerating) your rear tire in a curve.

But the story doesn't end here.

There's another piece of electronics called *Traction Control* that keeps your rear tire from spinning-out while accelerating.

Isn't this great news!

Traction Control uses the ABS sensors on both tires to detect when the rear tire starts to rotate faster than the front tire. When this state is detected, the system cuts power to the engine to prevent the rear wheel from spinning out. I'll explain Traction Control in a later chapter.

Here's the awesome truth: ABS and Traction Control can prevent certain types of crashes—and almost certainly save lives!

If this is true, why doesn't every motorcycle have them?

Good question. I'll attempt to answer that a little later.

WARNING: ABS and Traction Control can't overcome physics. If you're going around a curve faster than your tires can handle (or hit a slippery spot), you're going down. ABS and Traction Control don't give you more friction, but they do significantly reduce your chances of crashing.

And that's certainly great news!

FIFTY

Arguments Against ABS

If you've listened to the *Motorcycle Mentor Podcast*, you know I like to present both sides of every argument. I've already presented the *advantages* of ABS. In this chapter, I'll present the *disadvantages*.

Starting in 2012, all new cars and light trucks sold in the United States have come with ABS as standard equipment.

The technology is simple, mature, and relatively inexpensive.

So why haven't motorcycle manufacturers embraced ABS like the automotive industry?

Simple economics suggests it's because riders aren't demanding it.

Hopefully, this book will change a few minds.

Before we dive in, let me assure you that none of the arguments I'm about to present sway my strong belief that motorcycles equipped with ABS are significantly safer than motorcycles without.

ABS Disadvantage #1
The argument against ABS I hear most often is this.
"A friend said my first motorcycle shouldn't have ABS because it encourages poor braking habits."

My Thoughts:

ABS allows you to grab (squeeze) more brake than you could with conventional brakes. But just because you have ABS doesn't mean you will be forced to brake incorrectly. ABS doesn't change the way you brake; it just keeps you from locking up your tires.

The most important thing to know about motorcycle braking is that you should *predominantly use your front brake.* A bike without ABS won't teach you this, and it certainly won't slap you on the butt when you use your rear brake too much. The second most important thing to know about proper motorcycle braking is that you should *avoid locking up your rear tire.* ABS keeps you from doing this.

Proper braking techniques are first learned with your head and then developed with practice and repetition until the "correct way" becomes a part of your muscle memory.

This process is the same whether you have ABS or not.

Learn more about proper braking in *Motorcycle Smarts.*

ABS Disadvantage #2

The second argument against ABS I hear is this.
"Some riders can stop faster on a motorcycle without ABS than they can on the same motorcycle equipped with ABS."

My Thoughts:

This might be true for top riders. But while we would all like to believe we're in the top rider category, few of us are. I'm certainly not, and I presume you're not either. I'm not particularly motivated that MotoGP champion Valentino Rossi can stop faster *without* ABS.

I'm more moved that you and I can stop more quickly *with* ABS.

Every study I've seen shows that most riders (from beginning to experienced) can stop more quickly in panic situations with ABS than without it. As ABS technology improves, I predict that even MotoGP racers will use it. I promise they understand what's going to happen if their rear tire loses traction at 200 mph.

Hello, highside!

ABS Disadvantage #3
The third argument against ABS I hear is this.
"Motorcycles with ABS don't perform as well in dirt and gravel."

My Thoughts:
There's some truth to this argument, but it's not always the case. Some tests have shown that motorcycles with off-road ABS stop just as well or even better than their non-ABS cousins in off-road situations.[1]

Many adventure motorcycles, like the BMW R1200GS Adventure (my current bike), allow the rider to disengage the ABS.

Perfect. Turn ABS "off" when you go off-road—if you want to.

NOTE: I usually keep my ABS "on" even when I'm riding in off-road conditions. But that discussion is for another book.

The Bottom Line

I don't profess that current ABS technology is perfect. But the advantages—shorter stopping distances, fewer lowside and highside crashes, easier to use in panic stops—far outweigh the disadvantages. So much so that I've made a personal commitment never to own a modern bike that doesn't have ABS.

Just last week, I spotted a beautiful used Ducati ST4 for sale. The owner really wanted to sell it and marked it down to a great price.

I wanted it, but it didn't have ABS.

I had a serious conversation with myself and decided not to buy it.

I'll wait for one that has ABS.

Stop for a moment and think about it this way. If a car spinning out of control is coming across your lane in front of you, do you really want to worry about grabbing the *correct* amount of front and rear brake—the amount that stops you in the shortest distance but doesn't lock up your rear tire?

I don't ... and I won't ... because I have ABS.

I can grab both brakes and let ABS do its thing.

BMW embraced ABS before most others. When I started looking for my first motorcycle, the only used motorcycles with ABS in my price range (motorcycles old enough) were BMWs.

I didn't fully understand the advantages of ABS back then, so I ended up buying a motorcycle with conventional brakes.

BMW continues to lead the way. In 2013 BMW Motorrad was the first manufacturer to equip all new motorcycles with ABS as standard equipment. Way to go BMW.

ABS has been available on most touring and sport-touring bikes for years. Recently, other manufacturers (including Harley Davidson) have started offering models with ABS—sometimes as standard equipment and sometimes as an upgrade.

That's awesome!

I want my Harley friends
to have the same advantages I do.

FIFTY-ONE

Traction Control and Stability Control

Now that we understand the importance of ABS on motorcycles, let's talk about other electronics that can reduce your chances of crashing.

Recall that ABS keeps you from skidding your tires when braking (a leading trigger of lowside and highside crashes), but it doesn't keep you from spinning your rear tire when over-accelerating in a curve (also a trigger of lowside and highside crashes).

I have good news. *Traction Control* will.

Traction Control is an electronic system that prevents your rear tire from spinning (losing rotational contact with the asphalt) when accelerating. The system uses the ABS sensors to detect when your rear tire is slipping. When it does, it reduces torque to the rear wheel by cutting engine power.

Traction Control can also help you maintain control in low-speed situations like pulling out from a side street over a high lip of asphalt.

Remember, your rear tire has less friction once it starts spinning and wants to slide around to the side of least resistance.

QUICK TIP: If a motorcycle has Traction Control, it also has ABS. But just because a motorcycle has ABS doesn't mean it has Traction Control.

Here's where it gets a little confusing. There's another piece of electronics called *Stability Control* that helps you ride even more safely. Stability Control combines ABS, Traction Control, integrated brakes, and lean angle sensors into one system.

When the system senses that an *out-of-control state* is imminent (slide-out, over-acceleration, rear tire lock-up, etc.), it applies one or both brakes (and/or reduces engine power) to keep the bike stable.

Stability Control, sometimes also referred to as Electronic Stability Control (ESC) is like Traction Control on steroids.

Traction Control for MotoGP

MotoGP racers have experimented with Traction Control systems with mixed results. Some like it. Some don't. When asked what he thought about Traction Control, MotoGP champion Valentino Rossi said:

"Having the Traction Control system makes riding the motorcycle much easier and allows me to open the throttle more rapidly without launching me into a highside. Unfortunately, it takes away from the rider's natural ability and feel for the motorcycle, and makes it easier for people to compete with those who they couldn't before having this rider aide. It is basically cheating."[1]

At some point in the future, I predict we will all be riding motorcycles with Stability Control. When this happens, the naysayers—the same riders who don't have a clue what triggers lowside and highside crashes—will still be moaning that they don't need any electronic aids on their motorcycles.

In the end, it's your choice. Choose wisely.

QUICK TIP: It's important to remember that ABS, Traction Control, and Stability Control can't overcome the laws of physics. If you ride outside the limits of available friction, you will lose control. But most motorcycle crashes could have been avoided well within these limits. Remember what my motorcycle mentor used to tell me? TRUST YOUR TIRES.

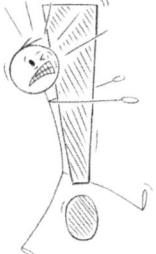 **Ride a motorcycle with Traction Control or Stability Control (both include ABS)—and say goodbye to most single-vehicle lowside and highside crashes.**

It's just that simple.

FIFTY-TWO

The Wrong Argument for ABS

Now that we've established that ABS is a beautiful thing, let's take a look at why some riders still don't see its benefits.

ABS proponents argue that ABS shortens their stopping distance, while anti-ABS proponents argue that top riders can stop more quickly with conventional brakes.

In this case, neither side wins because both sides are right.

We're losing the ABS debate because we're using the WRONG ARGUMENT!

The real reason I only ride motorcycles with ABS has nothing to do with stopping distances—and everything to do with crashing!

In my mind, the real benefit of ABS is that it ELIMINATES most lowside and highside crashes.

Another benefit I rarely hear mentioned is that riders with ABS feel less stress in panic stops because they don't have to worry about braking correctly. In other words, they can squeeze both brakes firmly without fear of locking up either tire.

This allows riders to focus more on avoiding the obstacle they're braking for in the first place.

According to an NHTSA study:

"Anti-lock brake systems not only prevent rider and motorcycle from harm and damage by increasing active safety, but also reduce significantly [the] mental strain while riding and braking. In case of a critical riding situation, this higher remaining mental reserve would help the rider to develop and wishfully realize alternative emergency strategies that additionally could help the rider to prevent a crash."[1]

NOW YOU KNOW THE REAL REASON I ONLY RIDE MOTORCYCLES WITH ABS.

Because riding one without ABS seems foolish.

FIFTY-THREE

A Case for Mandatory ABS

In *Motorcycle Smarts*, I was afraid to make this point. Not anymore.

By now, you know that I'm a huge proponent of ABS.

So much so that I think ABS should be federally mandated on all street motorcycles sold in the United States. There. I said it.

My hope is that it's already happened by the time you read this.

But just in case. Here's why.

ABS stops most riders more quickly than conventional brakes. But that's not the point I'm going to focus on because that's debatable and has lots of naysayers.

What's even more important to understand is that ABS keeps you from locking up your rear tire and triggering a rider-induced lowside or highside crash—every single time—even when you panic and apply both brakes as hard as you can.

I wrote the *Motorcycle Smarts* book series, in large part, to explain this so all riders and politicians can understand.

It's one of the most important points in this book.

Let me say it a different way.

I WOULD STILL CHOOSE TO RIDE A MOTORCYCLE WITH ABS EVEN IF IT MEANT IT TOOK ME A FEW FEET LONGER TO STOP THAN RIDERS WITH CONVENTIONAL BRAKES!

The physics explains all this with clarity.

There's no doubt in my mind that ABS would reduce the number of single-vehicle motorcycle crashes. There's no doubt in my mind ABS would lower the overall number of motorcycle fatalities.

Why is this point avoided in other motorcycle skills books?

I believe many riders don't see the need for ABS because their training didn't show them. And neither have the popular motorcycle skills books. If they had, I promise I wouldn't have felt the calling to write the *Motorcycle Smarts* series.

And neither have many of the federally funded crash studies.

The engineer in me says there must be huge opposition to mandatory ABS, or it would already be in place—like it is in Europe. But for the life of me, I can't imagine a viable argument against it.

This is why I explained lowside and highside crashes my way.

Could somebody please show Congress my explanations?

I'm sure folks argued against mandatory ABS for automobiles and light trucks too. But you found a way to pass that legislation.

It's time to do the same courtesy for motorcycle owners.

And while you're mandating ABS, why not go ahead and mandate Stability Control at the same time? The technology already exists.

If you have ABS and ESC (or Traction Control), you won't be able to spin your rear tire even if you give her too much throttle—further reducing the chances of triggering a lowside or highside crash.

At some point, maybe before you even read this book, I believe ABS *will* be mandatory. At that point, the purpose of this chapter is to convince riders that ABS, ESC, and Traction Control are good.

I know I won't be able to convince all of you.

I just spent my morning looking online at motorcycle forums, and there are certainly some passionate folks against ABS.

Maybe some of the same riders whose bike has never seen the rain?

If the naysayers would look past the stopping distance argument and instead focus on the fact that ABS prevents rider-induced lowside and highside crashes, I think some might reconsider.

If I convert one ABS naysayer, this book series was worth it.

In *Motorcycle Smarts,* I stopped short of recommending mandatory ABS. After studying the data for this book, I've changed my mind.

 Today. I'm asking Congress to pass legislation that requires ABS (and Stability Control) on all street motorcycles sold in the U.S.

You did this for cars in 2012. Are motorcyclists less important?

Europe passed ABS legislation years ago. It's time we do the same.

If you want to keep everyone happy, make it so riders can manually deactivate ABS when they want to—even though most never will.

I understand that if riders demanded ABS, manufacturers would already be providing it. That's not happening because no one seems to be talking about ABS preventing riders from triggering crashes.

The passionate arguments against ABS focus on stopping distances and the rider having full control (pop a testosterone pill, beat on chest) of his motorcycle without electronics getting in his way.

Give me a break.

Part Four: Riding Gear Hacks

Riding a motorcycle comfortably starts with having the right gear.

Unfortunately, I was slow to learn this for myself.

Somewhere along the way, I also learned that riding didn't have to be a battle of endurance—that there were things I could do when parts of my body hurt when I rode.

In this section, I'll share some tips about riding gear and ways you can ride more comfortably.

FIFTY-FOUR

Mother Nature up Close

Motorcycles put their passengers in the middle of Mother Nature.

In the spring, I love smelling freshly plowed ground and watching plants burst open in all shades of green.

The Yoshino Cherry tree is my favorite tree. It rewards those of us who will pause for long enough to notice with a delicate white bloom in the spring and an unmistakable fragrance in the fall.

I've never been able to find anything that confirms this, but they have an unusual scent in the fall that's unmistakable.

In early November, Elaeagnus shrubs perfume the afternoon sky in a magical way. The shrub grows like a weed and has thorns. I'm blessed that others around me have planted them so everyone can partake.

The Osmanthus Fragran shrub is also divine. It's dark green with a tiny white bloom. You'd never imagine a bloom so small could smell so intoxicating. One plant can perfume an entire block.

Enjoying Mother Nature is one of the best parts of riding.

Sometimes, I can't help but crack open my visor and smile.

FIFTY-FIVE

Gear Made for Motorcyclists

I'm ashamed to admit this, but during my first winter riding season, I wore a ski jacket and ski gloves. What a sight.

When I reached 35 mph, I puffed up like the Michelin man.

I know I must have looked like a dork.

One day, Fred gently suggested that a riding jacket might be more comfortable and offer more protection. I eventually listened.

At the time, I had no idea you could buy stuff that didn't flap in the wind. I just figured it was part of the pain of riding a motorcycle.

I was wrong.

When I rode for the first time in a riding jacket, I was amazed!

The jacket had a zipper and a flap that folded over it to keep the wind out. The same system was around my neck and both wrists. Who knew you could ride without air getting in? I didn't—until then.

Riding is so much more comfortable with the right gear. And that's not even factoring in the element of added crash protection.

As I kept riding, I purchased more and more stuff made specifically for folks on a motorcycle. I was amazed after every purchase.

My helmet keeps the wind and bugs away, and helps me if I crash.

My riding boots keep my feet warm and protect them if I crash. My riding jacket lets air in when I want it and keeps it out when I don't.

Then there was several pairs of summer gloves, earplugs, and riding pants with pads—and a more expensive riding jacket that had a liner I could zip in and out to match the weather.

AT EVERY STEP IN MY JOURNEY, I LEARNED THAT GEAR MADE SPECIFICALLY FOR MOTORCYCLISTS MADE ME MORE COMFORTABLE.

Longer rides became more enjoyable and less fatiguing.

Flapping became a thing of the past.

I also learned that more expensive gear is even better—lighter, more breathable, with better protection. Who knew?

Better helmets are quieter and have more air vents. Better riding boots keep my feet dry in the wet yet breathe so my feet don't sweat in the heat. I still don't understand how they do that. But they do.

And I have some amazing lower-priced finds that I wouldn't part with. My inexpensive foam earplugs give me mental peace and quiet. My side stand puck allows me to park on soft ground with confidence.

And my neck sock whatchamacallit keeps the knife-splitting air away from my neck when it's cold outside. You couldn't pry that away from me on a cold morning if you offered ten times what I paid for it.

My point here isn't that you get what you pay for. It's that riding gear made for motorcyclists will make your rides more comfortable.

And it only took me
like a year to figure that out.

FIFTY-SIX

Obsessing Over Riding Gear

One of the biggest mistakes I see new riders make is spending too much time obsessing over what riding gear to purchase.

I know this first hand. I did the same thing when I started.

Trust me. You'll want to change your riding gear soon—regardless of what you select to begin with. You'll learn more about what you like and don't like. You'll see new products that you didn't know existed. You'll learn what your riding buddies like and don't like.

Get a helmet (preferably DOT or Snell), a riding jacket (preferably bright with armor), and riding boots (preferably for motorcyclists).

Then you're done for a bit and can focus on your riding skills.

Granted, I enjoyed selecting my first riding jacket. But while I was studying to find the perfect one, I wore a dark blue winter coat that wasn't specifically made for motorcyclists.

During this period, I was hard to see, and I had no protection.

For what? I quickly replaced the first riding jacket I painstakingly selected with a riding jacket I liked better.

FIFTY-SEVEN

Earplugs Please

If only you would try earplugs for a week.

My motorcycle mentor Fred had a modest amount of hearing loss that he directly attributed to riding a motorcycle for so many years.

That caught my attention.

I have no idea if he was right, but I do know he encouraged me to give earplugs a try—and I did.

At first, I felt apprehensive about wearing them. I struggled to get them properly situated equally in both ears. One was always tighter than the other, which annoyed me. I'm like that.

But the thing that freaked me out was that I was apprehensive that if I was in a crash, I wouldn't be able to hear the paramedics watching over me. "Sir, can you move your toes." Nothing.

Both concerns got easier to manage because I got better at putting the plugs in and more aware that I could hear folks talking to me.

Now, I can't imagine riding a motorcycle without earplugs.

On my 8058-mile ride to Alaska with Mike, I rode maybe a couple of hundred miles without earplugs—just to break things up. For the other 7858 miles, I wore them. Nothing fancy. Just the foam ones.

Yes, they take some getting used to.

Yes, it takes some practice to put them in correctly.

Yes, they make riding so much more enjoyable.

I really think you should give them a try.
You'll hear thoughts inside your helmet, just like me.

FIFTY-EIGHT

Get a Tank Bag

The biggest mistake I made on my ride to Alaska was NOT having a tank bag. I could explain away my excuses, but that sounds boring.

My point here is that a tank bag is amazing—like one of the most enjoyable things I have on a motorcycle.

Basically, I get to have a purse, and that makes me giddy.

I put everything in there. Chargers, a flashlight, insurance and tag stuff, helmet rain finger squeegee, duct tape, neck warmer, a ball cap, pen and paper, pressure gauge, a little cash, earplugs, face shield wipes, tools, and an assortment of gloves. Plus, a lot more.

A man on a motorcycle can't have too many pairs of gloves.

All this to say, if you don't have a tank bag, you should give it a try. If your tank is metal, a magnetic bag will do fine. If it's not, you'll have to opt for a strap-on bag.

Just google your motorcycle and year with the term "tank bag," and you'll find sizing and mounting options.

You can thank me later.

FIFTY-NINE

Sticky Gloves

When I started riding, and every moment since, I've battled with my right hand getting fatigued while riding for long stretches.

I'm sure it's partly a mental thing, just knowing I can't let go of the throttle for more than a second.

None of my bikes so far have had electronic cruise control.

I mentioned this fatigue to my mentor Fred one day, and he asked me if my gloves were *snug* and *sticky*.

"What do you mean?" I asked.

"You don't have to squeeze nearly as hard to keep the throttle open when your glove material doesn't easily slide against your palm or grip.

As it turns out, I took Fred's advice and purchased a pair of gloves that was snug and sticky against my particular throttle grip.

Oh my gosh. I could immediately tell the difference!

My favorite pair of riding gloves is my favorite because I don't have to squeeze the grip much to keep the throttle open.

I have several pairs of winter gloves that aren't sticky or snug, and they require that I squeeze tighter to keep the throttle open. I can tell a big difference in hand fatigue.

Thanks Fred for another great tip.

SIXTY

My Fingers Go Numb

I rarely have a problem with my fingers tingling or going numb, but I know plenty of riders who do. It's real, and it's frustrating.

Honestly, I don't have enough data to prove this, but it seems like the folks who ride bikes that vibrate a lot are more prone to this.

If you struggle with tingling or numbness, here are some things to try.

First, you might want to give padded gloves a try. The padding is usually only on the palm side where your hand makes contact with the grips. I use them even though I don't struggle with numbness.

I just find them to be comfortable.

Recall in the last chapter when Fred told me to try gloves that were sticky and snug? Properly fitting gloves allow you to keep the throttle in the desired position without squeezing as hard.

A softer grasp on your grip will actually lower the vibrations that make it to your fingers/hand. This almost certainly reduces the likelihood of your fingers going numb.

Another option to consider if it's your throttle hand that has issues is some form of throttle assist.

Full Disclosure:

My mentor Fred thought anything that kept the throttle in the open position was dangerous.

Fred had a point. You'll need to evaluate that for yourself.

Even at that, I keep a device called a Crampbuster throttle assist on my motorcycle at all times. I still have to at least rest my hand on the throttle to keep it open, but I can do it without gripping it.

I love my Crampbuster—even though it's a simple piece of plastic.

Please don't tell Fred, but I also used a mechanical throttle assist on my ride to Alaska. I didn't use it much, but I loved being able to pull my right hand off the throttle for a few seconds.

If none of these solutions help, you might want to consider a different grip. This is especially true if both hands are tingling and going numb. Also, make sure the bar end weights are intact since they absorb some of the vibrations.

If you still can't find a solution, try riding different motorcycles to see if you have the same problems. If you don't have access to another motorcycle, consider renting one for a day. Money well spent. Numb hands are one of the ailments you should be able to remedy.

Life is too short to ride a motorcycle
with numb body parts.

SIXTY-ONE

My Back Hurts

When I started riding, the thing I worried about the most—second to crashing and leaving my kids without a dad—was back pain.

I broke my back moving a refrigerator when I was eighteen, and sitting in a chair with no back just about kills me even to this day. Isn't sitting on a motorcycle like sitting on a chair with no back?

Luckily, it isn't for me.

If you have more back pain while riding than you care to navigate, try adjusting your riding position as much as you can. Can you slide up (or back) in the seat? Can you adjust your grip positions?

Does your buddy's motorcycle hurt your back any less?

I've never tried one, but riders have told me that backrests rock.

But sometimes, the most effective way to alter your riding position is to change bikes. Over the years, each of my motorcycles felt drastically different after a long ride. None of them was perfect.

It's probably true for all of us that riding a motorcycle won't be as comfortable as riding in a car. But it shouldn't be so bad that we have to grin-and-bear-it through every mile. If it is, adjust something.

SIXTY-TWO

My Butt Hurts

Of all the discomforts of riding a motorcycle, butt pain is perhaps the one that a rider can fiddle with the most.

Let's make a distinction. Discomfort is one thing. Pain is another.

You can spot a rider with butt pain a mile away. He's squirming around on his motorcycle seat searching for relief. After squirming doesn't work, he signals to his buddies that he's getting low on gas—or needs a bathroom break—even though they stopped fifty miles back.

The good news is that motorcycle seats are bigger and usually more comfortable than bicycle seats. The bad news is—not by much.

Ouch.

NOT ALL BUTT PAIN IS THE SAME.

If your discomfort is more of a burning and itching skin irritation, then I have the perfect solution. It's called *Monkey Butt Powder*.

It's amazing and available online and at motorcycle retailers.

Monkey Butt Powder is an anti-moisture, anti-friction product you apply "down there" to keep your "hardware" dry as a desert.

It's particularly important when you're riding in hot weather, but the anti-friction advantages are real in all weather conditions. Give it all a good dusting, and you're good to go. You can thank me later.

Figure 62-1 Monkey Butt Powder

BUT DAVE! MY BUTT HURTS FROM THE PRESSURE POINTS OF SITTING ON SOMETHING SO SMALL.

No problem, let's talk through your options.

First, get out your wallet. These options cost more than powder.

The easiest and least expensive solution is to try a seat cushion that sets on top of your seat. There are tons of options here.

Several years back, I started using a seat cushion for long rides, and it makes a big difference. It's a bit tricky to keep it positioned correctly, but with practice, it's doable.

Another option to curb your butt pain while riding is to purchase an aftermarket seat that replaces your stock seat.

Believe it or not, stock motorcycle seats are almost always uncomfortable because they're too soft. Aftermarket seats are usually firmer.

I have a riding buddy who swears by them and has an aftermarket seat on all of his motorcycles.

RIDING POSITION

The riding position on a cruiser-type motorcycle places the rider in a feet-forward position. While this might look comfortable, it transfers more weight down through the rider's butt instead of their legs.

Compare this position to an adventure-type motorcycle where the rider's feet are directly below their body. In this position, more of the rider's weight is carried down to the foot pegs through their legs.

Think of it this way. Every pound that goes through a rider's legs is one less pound that has to be carried down through his butt.

Ironically, putting your feet on highway pegs is the worst position for butt pain. When your feet are dangling out in front of your body, *all* of your weight has to go down through your backside.

Perhaps these pegs should be called *anti-highway* pegs.

AND WHEN NOTHING ELSE WORKS

The bad news is that butt pain is real, and it's sometimes nearly impossible to mitigate on a particular bike. But the good news is that you have lots of other motorcycles to choose from.

Trust me. Every motorcycle I've owned felt different.

If you're new to motorcycles, I have to warn you. You're probably going to be at least a little uncomfortable on long rides if you weigh more than a few pounds.

It's just one of those things you'll have to manage.

You'll know when the
discomfort is too much.

SIXTY-THREE

My Neck Hurts

I've struggled with neck pain on every motorcycle I've owned.

My first motorcycle was a Honda VFR, and it put me in a forward riding position. This forced me to use the muscles in the back of my neck to hold my head upright. What made it even worse was that my neck wasn't yet conditioned to hold up the weight of a full face helmet.

As my neck got stronger, the discomfort mostly went away.

My second motorcycle had a large adjustable windscreen. It was so big that it deflected air over me and onto the *back* of my helmet.

I had to keep my neck muscles engaged when I was riding over 50 mph. This was very uncomfortable. I never could get that worked out and eventually sold it even though I loved everything about it but that.

And just to make the point that everyone fits differently, a riding buddy had the same motorcycle, and he never had any neck discomfort. Perhaps I was taller, or shorter, or had longer arms. I have no idea.

All I know is that I couldn't get comfortable on it, so I sold it.

Every rider is different. Every motorcycle is different. How you fit on your bike will be unique to your body dimensions.

If your neck hurts when you ride, here are some things to try.

First, give your body some time to acclimate to a different riding position. To this day, my neck bothers me if I haven't ridden much in a while. Give it some time, and you might be fine.

My mentor told me that air hitting me while riding would be one of the most fatiguing parts of my journey. He also told me that trying to control *it* would be one of the most challenging things I did.

He was right on both counts—again.

CAN SOMEONE SAY WINDSCREEN?

A big factor in how the air hits you is your windscreen.

Some screens direct the air into your chest. Some screens direct the air over your body. But you don't get something for nothing. Some of the taller screens deflect so much air that they create turbulence.

The windscreen on one of my motorcycles tossed my head around like a bobblehead doll. I eventually got used to it.

If you don't like the way your windscreen is doing its thing, find a different one. Look online for suggestions for your particular bike and body type. You might be surprised at how many owners are struggling with the same issue.

CAN SOMEONE SAY HELMET?

I never believed that changing helmets would change how my neck felt until I tried it. Different helmets also change how the air moves your head around—which also affects neck discomfort.

It's worth a try, isn't it?

Buying a different helmet is cheaper than buying a different bike. Another thing to consider is that generally speaking, more expensive helmets are lighter within the same classification. And a lighter helmet might relieve some of the discomfort in your neck.

Ed Becker, Executive Director of the Snell Foundation that tests motorcycle helmets, once told me that helmet makers build different size helmets with the same outer shell.

In other words, your particular helmet model might be made with the same sized outer shell as a larger (or smaller) model. Whereas the same size helmet in another brand (or model) might be made with a smaller (lighter) outer shell.

Having learned this, you'll probably want to compare the weight of your helmet to other models and choose accordingly.

CAN SOMEONE SAY MOTORCYCLE?

As I mentioned earlier, I could never get comfortable on my ST1300. I loved the bike but hated how it fatigued my neck.

Life's too short. I sold it and bought something else.

---

*My neck is hurting right now just
thinking about that motorcycle.*

SIXTY-FOUR

Be Prepared

As a little boy, I never made it past Cub Scouts.

But I seem to recall that the Boy Scout's motto was *Be Prepared.*

This is great advice and something that all riders should follow. At a minimum, every rider should be prepared for hot, cold, rain, and fog on every ride. Ride for very long, and you'll get caught out in weather different than what was predicted. It's a given.

Don't get me wrong. I'm not suggesting you carry your warmest riding jacket in the middle of summer or your lightest summer riding jacket in the middle of winter.

What I am suggesting is you prepare for the unexpected.

At certain times of the year, temperatures can drop 20 degrees in a short period of time. What would happen if you broke down or had to take an unexpected route home which pushed your ride into darkness?

Trust me. You'll miss the warmth of the afternoon sun.

Be prepared for hotter weather too. It's bad to get stuck in the heat with riding gear designed for the cold.

Heat exhaustion is just as real as hypothermia.

And what about unexpected precipitation? It's going to happen.

You don't have to carry your Aerostich (ride in a monsoon) jacket, but you need something that offers some rain protection just in case.

I have a compact rain jacket that fits nicely in my tank bag.

I've used it many times.

For me, if my hands hurt, my entire body is uncomfortable—and gloves don't take up much space—so I take pairs that offer protection from the rain and comfort a little colder and hotter than I expect.

If your full face helmet has a tinted visor, carry one that's clear in case you get caught riding in the dark.

And make sure you know how to swap it.

The farther you travel from home, the more you need to prepare for the unexpected. If you're riding close to home, the unexpected can be handled by sucking it up and heading home.

If you're riding to Alaska, you pull over, put on the best gear you brought, and you keep going.

BEING PREPARED FOR THE UNEXPECTED IS A CRITICAL PART OF RIDING A MOTORCYCLE COMFORTABLY AND SAFELY.

Part Five: How-To Hacks

Sometimes it's good to know what to do before you have to do it.

In this section, I'll share hacks that cover topics like how to tame the wind, how to handle a dead battery, and how to ride on gravel.

I'll also give you some tips on how to find a motorcycle mentor.

SIXTY-FIVE

I Finally Dropped Her

I didn't much like it when folks used to tell me it was just a matter of time before I dropped my motorcycle. I guess they were right.

The ride started out perfectly—mid-60s with autumn all around.

After a long breakfast with a riding buddy, I headed out for a solo ride through Mother Nature. Frankly, I had no idea where I was going, but that's the way I wanted it.

I'd read that Alabama has a great collection of old covered bridges, but I had never seen one in my car. I guess it makes sense that major roads bypass those sorts of things in the name of making-good-time.

I had no place to go and no time to be there.

I was on county road something, headed west. Out of the corner of my eye, I saw "Clarkson Covered Bridge" with an arrow pointing to the right. I firmly squeezed the front brake on my VFR and made the right-handed turn. The bridge was a mile down on the right.

On a normal day, the view would have been just okay, but today it was amazing—with orange leaves everywhere. It felt like a postcard.

I pulled up to the bridge, got off my motorcycle, and proceeded to take advantage of the near-perfect photo op.

After several pictures, I decided that an even better shot would be if my bike was a few feet to the left. I lifted the side stand and rolled her over. Then I leaned it over to dismount.

To my surprise, instead of stopping at the normal side stand angle, she kept going. Before my brain could send a signal to my left leg to *hold that positio*n, it was too late. I knew I didn't stand a chance.

All I could think was, "I hope this doesn't hurt."

In an attempt to save my leg, I not-so-gracefully fell to the ground beside her. A quick assessment yielded no broken bones, and a quick scan yielded no onlookers. I began to laugh out loud.

———

Fortunately, I was able
to pick her up by myself.

SIXTY-SIX

How to Clean Your Face Shield

Sometimes I wonder if I missed my life's calling.

I love comparing stuff, and working for Consumer Reports magazine would have been a blast.

When I was in the 7th grade, I did a Science Project on batteries.

I compared the cost versus performance of Duracell and Energizer alkaline batteries, along with standard (non-alkaline) batteries.

I measured how long each battery could power my favorite flashlight, then divided the cost by the run time to see which one was the most economical.[*]

Thirty years later, I did a comparison early in my riding career to see which cleaning solution worked best on my helmet face shield.

I tried the following options: Windex with a paper towel, Windex with newspaper, and soap and water with a paper towel.

My experiment lacked real scientific controls, but I never intended to publish my results. Instead, I simply wanted to know which method worked best for me. Why not do your own test? Science can be fun.

I hesitate to share my results because I'm not sure you would come to the same conclusions—and some say Windex can scratch plastic.

But here goes anyway.

The *Windex with paper towel* performed well. With a little effort, I was able to clean bug guts off the outside of my shield and crud off the inside. I could smell the Windex in my helmet for a few minutes after I cleaned it, but this wasn't a big deal to me.

The *Windex with newspaper* did about the same as the *Windex with paper towel.* The newspaper didn't leave any lint on the shield, but it did leave newsprint all over my hands—super annoying.

The *soap and water with paper towel* option performed surprisingly well. Overall, it cleaned the bugs off the outside of the shield with less effort than the Windex solution.

Conclusions

It's hard to beat the simplicity of Windex sprayed on a sheet of paper towel, but I found that the soap and water option performed better.

Cheap, effective, simple—and always in hand. The perfect mix.

To make things simple, I keep several paper towels pre-moistened with a soap and water solution (Dawn dish soap is my preference) in a Ziploc bag inside my tank bag.

I always have access to these when I'm on the road.

As an added test, I took saliva and newspaper and wiped the inside of my face shield. You may have heard that wiping spit on the inside of water goggles helps keep them from fogging up.

I wanted to test this for myself, and here's what I learned.

Wiping spit on the inside of my helmet was gross. On top of that, I found that the half of the shield cleaned with soap and water alone was less likely to fog up than the side with saliva. Myth busted.

––––––––

In my Science Fair Project, I found that Duracell Coppertop batteries performed the best—factoring in runtime and cost. Even though that was in 1972, I still prefer Duracell batteries over Energizer.

SIXTY-SEVEN

How to Tame the Wind

Fred always told me that the air rushing around me would be one of the most fatiguing parts of riding a motorcycle. He was right.

On my first motorcycle, a Honda VFR, at speeds over 50 mph, the aerodynamics of the shield and bike bounced my head around like the little plastic ball in a lottery machine.

Riding for more than a few miles was exhausting.

I tried different shields but never found the perfect solution. One shield directed air at my chest, but it was just as fatiguing. I even tried a tiny shield but decided that I preferred more protection.

Once I learned there were worse solutions, I went back to the original shield that made my head bobble. That would be good enough.

Every bike I've owned has had its own way of fatiguing me.

As I explained earlier, my Honda ST1300 had the largest and most adjustable shield of any motorcycle I've owned, but I never could get comfortable riding it.

Fighting the air around me has always been a challenge.

But just because a particular motorcycle or shield is fatiguing to me doesn't mean it will be to you.

Every motorcycle fits every rider a little differently.

At first glance, touring bikes with a big screen (like the Goldwing) seem like they would be the most comfortable to ride. Right?

Not necessarily.

A shield doesn't block the air. It diverts it. Air flows around the shield but comes back together at some point. Different shields divert the air in different patterns based on their shape and size.

Some shields, like the GIVI I had on my Honda VFR, curve up. This is good and bad. The shield pushed the air up higher, so I could see over, but it deflected air into the top of my helmet. If I was two inches shorter, this shield might have been perfect for me.

Here are five things you can try to reduce fatigue.

1. Try earplugs.

Along the way, I discovered that air rushing around me is loud and creates pressure differences. These pressure differences not only bobble my head around, but they also generate low-frequency sounds.

Everything instantly got better when I started wearing earplugs.

My first ride with earplugs was much less fatiguing, not because I changed the way air hit me, but because I blocked out some of the noise that it created. I can't overemphasize how much more enjoyable riding became when I started wearing earplugs.

2. Try a different shield.

A quick Google search will reveal tons of shields that will fit your motorcycle. Consider an adjustable shield if you can find one.

3. Try a different helmet.

Some helmets are more aerodynamic and handle wind buffeting better than others. Ask around at your local bike shop for suggestions.

4. Be patient and persistent.

Be patient and persistent as you step through the process.

You CAN make things better, but in the end, you have to realize (like I did) that you're on a motorcycle.

5. TRY A DIFFERENT MOTORCYCLE.

Have you ridden other motorcycles that were less fatiguing? Try to figure out why. Was the faring smaller (naked), or was it larger?

Was the shield big or small? If you can answer these questions, it will help you select a bike that fits your body.

Based on the large number of after-market shields on the market, we're not the only ones looking for relief.

The challenge remains …

What works for me might not work for you. And regardless of what you do, you'll still have air rushing around you

---

Fred was right. Taming the wind is tricky.

SIXTY-EIGHT

How to Find Neutral

Finding neutral in my driveway never seems to be a problem.

Finding neutral at the ATM with ten cars behind me is different.

Getting your motorcycle into neutral can be tricky—especially on some bikes. My Honda VFR was the worst.

I used to work on an Army installation that required everyone to stop and show their badge before proceeding. One time when I went through, I couldn't get my motorcycle in neutral. I finally had to turn it off so I could use both hands to present my badge.

A long line of impatient drivers behind me didn't help.

It was then that I decided I needed a surefire way to get my bike in neutral—especially at guard gates and toll booths.

This is the hack I came up with.

What I figured out for my VFR (and every bike I've owned since) is that it always goes into neutral more easily if I'm rolling when I shift up from first gear.

So, when I'm next in line at the ATM, I wait for a second to let the car in front of me clear. Then, I put my bike in first gear and pull up toward the machine. While I'm still rolling, I pull in the clutch and pop the gear shifter up from first into neutral.

It works like a charm every time.

This procedure takes some thinking because you'll need enough speed to carry you all the way to the ATM without engine power. But you don't need all that much because you'll be close.

With a little practice, you'll figure out what works best for you.

The trick is to shift up while you're still rolling.

If your bike is easy to get into neutral, you're probably wondering why I wrote an entire chapter on something so simple.

But not all motorcycles are the same.

SIXTY-NINE

How to Handle No Starts

It's just a matter of time before this is you.

You suit up, mount your bike, flip up the side stand, turn the key to the "on" position, pull in the clutch, and hit the starter button.

And nothing happens.

You release the starter button, say a quick prayer, and hit it again.

And the starter still doesn't engage.

Thoughts of "oh crap" rush through your mind.

How am I going to get home? What should I do next?

Trust me. This has happened to me many times, and I was able to start it just fine with a little troubleshooting.

NOTE: The guidelines below are for most modern motorcycles.

CAN SOMEONE SAY DEAD BATTERY?

Since you probably suspect a bad battery at first, let's look at that first.

The great thing about batteries is that they tell us when they're dead.

And the easiest way for your battery to tell you there's a problem is with a weak horn. If it fails to make a sound or sounds wimpy, you probably have a dead battery.

If your horn sounds strong, it's probably not your battery that's keeping the starter from engaging.

In some ways that's good news. In some ways, it's not.

Another indicator of your battery strength is the brightness of your headlight. This can be a little tricky to check because on some motorcycles, the headlight doesn't come on until the bike is running.

On other bikes, it comes on when you turn the key "on" but goes off when you engage the starter.

In any case, if your headlight is strong, even for a few seconds, it's a good indicator that your battery is fine. If your headlight comes on but looks dim, you probably have a dead battery.

If it's your battery, take a look at the next chapter for what to do next. Here, let's assume your horn and headlight are both strong—which indicates that your battery is fine.

CAN SOMEONE SAY KILL SWITCH?

The next thing to check is to make sure the kill switch on the right bar hasn't been flipped. For me, this sometimes happens when I place my helmet on the handlebars while I'm gearing up.

If it's in the "kill" position, just flip it back, and you're good.

If it's in the "run" position, let's keep troubleshooting.

CAN SOMEONE SAY SIDE STAND SWITCH?

Since most motorcycles will start when the side stand is in the "down" position *if the motorcycle is in neutral,* go ahead and pull the side stand up, pull in the clutch, and put the motorcycle in neutral.

When you do this, you're eliminating some switch logic issues and stacking the odds in your favor that your motorcycle will start.

The side stand switch logic on most modern motorcycles is important but tricky. When the side stand is in the "down" position, and the motorcycle is in gear (even if you have the clutch pulled in), the starter is prevented from engaging.

Similarly, if you start your motorcycle with your side stand in the "down" position (only possible because your bike is in neutral), it will immediately go dead if you try to put the bike into gear.

This is actually a great safety feature!

It prevents you from taking off with the side stand in the "down" position. On older bikes, riders crashed because they rode off with the side stand "down." Right turns were okay. Left turns were not.

I suppose enough riders crashed this way for engineers to add the switch and the logic to prevent the engine from running when the side stand is in the "down" position when it's in gear.

Most modern motorcycles will NOT start or run when it's in gear and the side stand is in the 'down' position—even if the clutch is engaged.

So, if your bike starts fine but dies when you put it into gear, even though the side stand is in the "up" position, there's likely a problem with your side stand switch.

Unfortunately, these switches can be troublesome. Crud can get in there, and even a small misalignment can activate the logic. That's why I suggested you put the bike in neutral as part of your troubleshooting —to effectively bypass the side stand switch logic.

BUT DAVE, THE BATTERY SEEMS FINE AND THE STARTER STILL WON'T ENGAGE!

Okay, there is one more thing you can check before you throw in the towel. I'm only mentioning this because I've made this mistake.

Are you sure the key isn't in the "accessory" position?

Just to make sure, put your bike in neutral (green light on), pull in the clutch, lift the side stand to the "up" position, and hit the starter button in every key position. After you've done this, put the key into the "run" position and try one last hail mary.

Flip the kill switch to the "other" position.

I've made that mistake, too—thinking the "run" position was actually the "kill" position! I doubt I'm the only rider who's done that.

I'm glad my embarrassing moments could help.

If your battery is strong and your starter still won't engage, you've at least isolated the problem and know it's not user error. Keep reading.

SEVENTY

How to Handle a Dead Battery

Let's say you've determined you have a battery problem. Now what?

In some ways, a dead battery is simple in that you have a couple of straightforward options that will likely get you on your way.

You can jump-start it.

You can replace it.

You can get a tow.

You can push-start it.

As I mentioned in the last chapter, when your starter won't engage, it's oftentimes something other than your battery. In this chapter, let's assume you've determined you have a weak battery.

Here, your options are pretty straightforward.

CAN SOMEONE SAY JUMP-START IT?

The great thing about motorcycles is that they use 12-volt batteries like automobiles. This means you can jump-start your motorcycle with a car—same jumper cables and all.

If you have one of those compact emergency batteries for your car that will jump-start it, you can use it on your motorcycle too.

It's worth the money to keep one on your bike. I pack one on long trips. I should probably keep one on my bike all the time.

I'll go over how to jump-start your motorcycle in the next chapter.

CAN SOMEONE SAY REPLACE IT?

In full disclosure, I seem to have battery problems before big rides—and it's totally my fault.

When Mike and I left for the Mid Atlantic Backcountry Discovery Route (MABDR) several years ago, my battery pooped out three miles away from my house when I was getting gas.

Mike, the planner on the team, had a spare battery and brought it to me. We changed it out in the parking lot and went on our way.

I bought him a new battery when we got back. Mike never gave me a hard time for ignoring the warning signs of a dead battery.

He never said:

"That time I had to bale you out with a battery."

"That time you left for our trip with a dead battery."

"That time you didn't prepare for a long ride like you should have."

Now you know why I picked Mike to ride to Alaska with.

All that to say, it's not hard to replace a battery in a parking lot. You just need a battery and a few tools to loosen the battery terminals. And you need to know how to get to your battery—which almost always requires that you remove the seat.

CAN SOMEONE SAY GET A TOW?

I know this might sound extreme, but just so you know—you can call a wrecker when you need your motorcycle moved from point A to point B. It's not always pretty, though.

The key here is that you need to tell the wrecker service that it's for a motorcycle. This likely means that they will bring a flatbed wrecker. The second thing you need to know is that if the driver doesn't secure your bike properly, it's going to fall over on its side during the tow.

I saw this first-hand when my riding buddy needed a tow after he lowside crashed. The tow truck driver didn't secure the front tires in a wheel chock, and his Triumph fell on its side within a few miles.

Since the bike was totaled, it didn't much matter. But if it wasn't, it would have felt totally different.

CAN SOMEONE SAY PUSH-START IT?

Honestly, I've had mixed results trying to push-start my motorcycle.

At best, it's exhausting. At worst, it's not going to work.

The procedure to push-start a motorcycle is similar to that of push-starting a car. I'll cover that in more detail in a later chapter.

Keep reading.

SEVENTY-ONE

How to Jump-Start Your Motorcycle

Before you attempt to jump-start your bike, be sure your battery is the problem. If your horn and lights are strong, your battery is fine.

Jump-starting a motorcycle is just like jump-starting a car.

You'll need a battery source: an automobile, another motorcycle, or a portable battery pack—and a set of regular jumper cables.

Once the batteries are close enough for the jumper cables to reach, take the cables and connect the good battery to the bad one—making sure not to allow the cable ends to touch each other.

Connect the positive terminals (+) together with the red cable.

Connect the negative terminals (-) together with the black cable.

NOTE: To reduce the risks, it's safer to connect the jumper cables in the following order:
1. Red cable to positive (+) terminal on dead battery.
2. Red cable to positive (+) terminal on good battery.
3. Black cable to negative (-) terminal on good battery.
4. Black cable to negative (-) terminal on bad battery.
*** *It's a circle: dead red, good red, good black, bad black.*

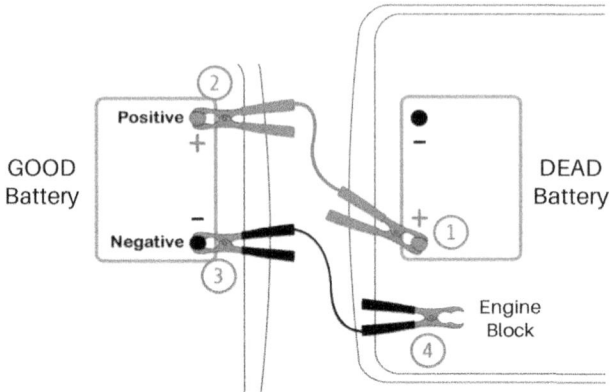

Figure 71-1 How to Jump-Start a Dead Battery

Want to reduce your risks even more?

Instead of making the last connection to the negative terminal on the dead battery, connect it to a metal piece on the motorcycle frame.

See Figure 71-1 (above).

This is because there's usually a spark when you make that connection, and it's best to keep that away from the battery.

Having said this, I've rarely been successful jump-starting a vehicle when I made the last connection to the frame instead of the negative battery terminal. But it's worth a try. I thought I should mention it.

First Attempt

Make sure the key is in the "run" position, and it's in neutral.

This will bypass the side stand sensor logic we discussed earlier.

Without starting the donor vehicle with a good battery, try to start your motorcycle. If it doesn't have enough juice to spin the starter, wait another minute and try again.

Once it starts, disconnect the batteries in the reverse order that you connected them. If it still won't start, continue below.

Second Attempt

This time, start the engine on the donor vehicle.

Turn off all electrical equipment and give it a little gas to increase the engine speed to 2500 RPMs. Hold it there for 30 seconds, and try to start your bike again.

If it won't start, wait another minute and try it once more.

Once it starts, disconnect the batteries in the reverse order that you connected them. If it still won't start, continue below.

Third Attempt

Let's give it one more try before we throw in the towel.

First, if you have the negative jumper cable connected to the frame of your motorcycle, reposition that cable to the negative terminal on your motorcycle battery. As I mentioned earlier, I've had much better success connecting the cable directly to the battery.

Next, make sure both cables are connected as securely as possible to the four battery terminals.

If they aren't, no number of attempts is going to work here.

Next, repeat what you did on the last attempt. Increase the RPMs on the donor vehicle and hold it there for a minute or so. Then try to start your bike. If it won't start, wait another minute and try again.

Once it starts, disconnect the batteries in the reverse order that you connected them. If it still won't start, continue below.

BUT DAVE, IT STILL WON'T START.

If it still won't turn over, you might have a shorted-out battery or a bad starter—or something worse.

At this point, your options are to replace the battery, have it towed, or call a friend with a motorcycle trailer.

Sure. I suppose you could try to push-start it. But why?

If your battery is so bad that you weren't able to jump-start it, it's unlikely you'll be successful push-starting it.

Either way, I'll cover that next.

SEVENTY-TWO

How to Push Start Your Motorcycle

Push-starting your motorcycle isn't as hard as running a marathon.

But it sure can feel close. Okay, I can't really make that comparison because I've never run a marathon. But you get my point.

Maybe I'm overstating the difficulty, but after the handful of times I've done it, I was panting like a dog in no time—and I had help.

Why is push-starting your motorcycle the last option I describe?

Push-starting your bike doesn't have to be your last option. If you don't have jumper cables or a donor vehicle, say you're somewhere by yourself, then push-starting your motorcycle makes perfect sense.

THE PROCEDURE

To push-start your motorcycle, try to find a downhill slope.

NOTE: Don't pick a slope so steep that you can't push it back up. It's best to assume you'll need more than one try to get it started—mostly because you'll likely need more than one try to get it started.

Any slope is better than no slope. Gravity is a good thing. It's also best to be on solid ground—concrete or asphalt instead of dirt.

NOTE: If it's warm outside and your motorcycle has been running, it will be easier to push-start it than if it's 20 degrees and it hasn't run in weeks. Again, I know this from personal experience. I never could get it push-started that day. I ended up jump-starting it just fine.

Once you get your bike up the hill, you're ready to go. You can do all this by yourself, but if you see anybody close by that looks capable of jogging, ask them (beg them) for help. Are you ready?

1. Position your motorcycle heading downhill.
2. Turn the key to the "run" position. Double-check and triple-check this. The motorcycle won't start in the accessory position. How do I know? *I'd rather not say.*
3. Mount the motorcycle like you're going to ride it.
4. Pull up the side stand, pull in the clutch, and put the motorcycle into second gear.
5. Take a deep breath and say a quick prayer for help.
6. Now, run like hell (while still straddling it), propelling the motorcycle as fast as you can. Sure, you'll look like a dork, but that's the way it has to be. If you have a helper, have him push from the back.
7. When you can't run any faster, or you can't breathe any harder, sit down and put your feet on the pegs.
8. Next, yell to your partner to let go and then release the clutch for a second or two. Don't leave the clutch out the entire time, or it will stop your motorcycle too fast. If the motorcycle starts, pull in the clutch and give it some gas. Whatever you do, don't let the engine die after it starts.
9. If it didn't start and you're still rolling, continue to release the clutch in quick bursts to spin the engine.

BUT DAVE, IT DIDN'T START.

If it didn't start, you can throw in the towel or give it another go.

To do this, you'll need to push it back up the hill. Now would be a great time to offer to buy lunch for your helper if they'll go again.

> NOTE: I'm convinced it's harder to push-start a motorcycle with a *dead* battery than one with a *weak* battery. This comes from personal experience and the fact that most modern motorcycles need some power to fire the spark plugs and run the fuel pump. If your battery is totally dead, your first few attempts will mostly supply a little juice to the battery to power these things. If this is true, the good news is that the second attempt might be more successful.

BUT DAVE, IT STILL DIDN'T START ON THE SECOND ATTEMPT?

Okay, I get that push-starting a motorcycle can be exhausting and that you might want to give up. But if you're okay to give it one more shot —maybe because it almost started on the last attempt—go for it.

This time, as an option, you could try first gear instead of second. A lower gear ratio will increase the turn-over speed of the engine, but it will also bleed your speed faster. In other words, when you release the clutch, it's going to feel like you're applying the brakes.

Another thing to keep in mind is that when it starts, it's going to pull hard, so be ready to pull in the clutch.

Here comes the engineer in me.

If your battery is shorted out, you won't be able to push-start or jump-start your motorcycle. This is because there's an open circuit in the battery, and the electronics won't be able to get power.

If your battery is shorted, you'll need to replace it.

SOMETIME LATER

When the dust settles and you're back home safely, you'll want to ask yourself, "Why was my battery dead?"

If you know the reason, like you left your bike "on," that's actually good. You can feel confident that your motorcycle will start fine once the electrical system has a chance to charge the battery.

If you can't explain why the battery was dead, something is wrong. It's probably just a bad battery that needs to be replaced.

If you're not sure,
have a technician take a look.

SEVENTY-THREE

How Not to Leave Your Bike at Lunch

It was a beautiful fall day, and we decided to ride to lunch.

The leaves had just started to change colors, so my riding buddies and I picked a place over Monte Sano Mountain.

The views were spectacular. The air was cool and crisp, the sky was a magnificent blue, and the clouds were white like cotton.

I was so excited about the beauty around me, I suppose, that I left my motorcycle key in the "on" position when we went inside to eat.

I'd never done that before—and I've never done that since.

But on that particular day, I did.

When I returned to my bike, the battery had just enough juice left to make the headlight glow a faint orange. The horn sounded pathetic. My riding buddies laughed—and so did I.

"Help me push-start it," I said.

I figured it would be a piece of cake. Surely, three guys could push-start my medium-sized motorcycle without breaking a sweat.

I was wrong.

Granted, we didn't have a lot of room in the parking lot, but after three unsuccessful attempts, I thought:

"This is embarrassing."

At least the onlookers got a good laugh.

FINALLY

After each attempt, the headlight got a little stronger, and we could see that we were making progress—charging the battery bit by bit.

On the fourth attempt, the engine fired, and I immediately pulled in the clutch. I was exhausted and relieved. So were my aging friends.

I learned a valuable lesson that day.

*It's good to have a riding buddy or two
who can help push.*

SEVENTY-FOUR

How to Handle Gravel

Seeing gravel makes me pucker up in a flash.

I immediately think of two words: NO FRICTION.

I know this is extreme, but I imagine that I'm riding on ice.

All gravel isn't the same. There are jagged pieces that are made to semi-lock together. There are pea-sized pieces that roll like marbles.

Then there's gravel by itself and gravel scattered on a hard surface.

This is the type that puckers me the most, especially in a curve.

A light dusting of gravel on an asphalt parking lot was the culprit when I dropped my motorcycle in Utah on the way back from Alaska. I didn't notice the gravel, and my foot slid out in an instant.

But there's even more to consider.

Gravel on top of an asphalt road surface when you're going straight is one thing. Gravel on a road surface in a curve is worse.

Physics says your bike needs more friction when it's leaned over in a turn changing directions than when it's going in a straight line.

Your best option is to avoid gravel. But that's obviously not always possible. If that's not an option, imagine that you're riding on ice.

Be gentle on the throttle and brakes—and easy in the turns.

If you find gravel on a road surface in a straight line, ride straight through it. If you find it in a curve, you'll have to decide what to do next in a fraction of a second.

If there's a place in the road that doesn't have gravel, you could try to roll over that spot. If it's over the entire road, your best bet is to slow down and try not to use the part with gravel to make your turn.

In other words, be going straight as much as possible while you're rolling over the patch of gravel. Every scenario will be different. You'll need to pick a strategy in an instant—which makes this even harder.

Mike and I encountered this exact thing near the Canadian border on our ride to Alaska. Gravel dusted a newly paved road—in a curve.

As I recall, I was in the lead and noticed it first.

I slowed down and found a line without any gravel and called out to Mike in my helmet.

"Mike, there's gravel in the curve!"

Fortunately, we both made it through without going down.

What I remember most about that moment is that it happened so fast. I had to decide right then what I was going to do.

Now you know why seeing gravel puckers me up so fast.

Every. Single. Time.

SEVENTY-FIVE

How to Find a Good Motorcycle Mentor

I wish everyone who rides could have my motorcycle mentors.

Obviously, that's not possible. So, let's talk through a few characteristics you might want to look for in a good one. Since I'm moving at a brisk pace, let's jump right in, shall we?

Here are three questions you should ask a potential mentor.

Question One: How long have you been riding?

If they've been riding for less than three years—NO.

Question Two: What are your thoughts on using your rear brake?

If they say they predominately use their rear brake—NO. If they say locking up their rear tire triggers crashes—automatic YES.

Question Three: What is target fixation?

If they don't know—NO.

Obviously, this is a simple test, but I don't have the space to elaborate on a long list of questions. The ones above are good enough.

Just recognize this. Everyone who's ridden for a long time without crashing isn't necessarily a good mentor. Neither is someone who made it to Alaska and back on two wheels without dying.

You'll need to look for deeper characteristics than that.

Part Six: More Riding Hacks

I really hope you're enjoying this book so far!

In this section, I'll share some more riding tips that my motorcycle mentors shared with me—along with ones that I discovered for myself.

Thanks for following along.

SEVENTY-SIX

Dude's in My Helmet

Several years ago …

Mike wants to purchase headsets so we can talk while we're riding, but I don't like that idea so much.

I'm sure he's noticed my lack of interest and has wondered why I change the subject every time he brings it up.

It's because I enjoy the solitude and peace inside my helmet. Sometimes I ride to escape my normal life. I don't want to hear voices of my wife, my kids, or my boss. I don't want to hear my cell phone making noises that I just received an email notifying me of a once-in-a-lifetime opportunity to purchase a deeply discounted item online.

I like thinking private thoughts inside my helmet.

I like the comfort of talking to myself.

And sometimes, I like silence.

I'M NOT READY TO LET SOMEONE ELSE INSIDE.

Months later ...

On a ride to Arkansas, Mike pulled out two helmet headsets. One for him, and one for me. I tried not to look mortified. He was giddy.

"Hand me your helmet, and I'll put it in for you."

At that moment, I knew I was stuck.

I handed him my helmet and started praying it wouldn't fit.

He's an engineer, too, and had them configured in minutes.

———

The next morning after we geared up, Mike did a voice check.

"Can you hear me, Dave?"

At that moment, I realized I was screwed. Mike was going to hear me talk inside my helmet. Would he still want to be friends?

I couldn't be sure.

Earplugs in, helmet on, gloves on.

"Voice check, Dave. Can you hear me?"

For the first time in my life, I had allowed someone to get inside my helmet with me, and it didn't feel right. I waited as long as I could — and then reluctantly responded,

"Yes, I hear you. Can you hear me?"

At that moment, my life changed forever. I wanted to throw it on the ground to see if I could break that thing he just put in it. I thought about beating my head against the concrete when he wasn't looking.

I wonder what Mike would think if it mysteriously fell off?

Oh wait, don't ask that question out loud. He can hear you now.

See how this messes me up?

SOLITUDE
PLEASE!

We rode for another 120 miles or so, and I spoke more words than I wanted. I had someone else in there with me, and it felt weird.

At one point, I longed for solitude.

"Mike, I'm going to lay back to see how far these things reach."

We lost communication about a half mile later. I took several deep breaths and enjoyed the silence. Oh, sweet silence. It felt so good.

The solitude of being solo inside my helmet was back. I smiled.

Then with no warning, a female voice from the headset said:

"Rider 'A' has lost communication."

Darn near made me crash. What have I done? Now I've allowed a woman in there with me too!

Minutes later, Mike was back:

"Hey Dave. Can you hear me?"

"Yes. Can you hear me?"

Later that night at dinner, Mike confirmed my worst fears.

"Dave, I thought the headsets were awesome! We should use them when we ride to Alaska."

How do I get past this? How do I tell him what I really think?

I've got it. I'll tell this story in one of my books!

SEVENTY-SEVEN

Loud Pipes Save Lives Is
a Horrible Myth

The notion that loud pipes save lives has never impressed me.

At best, it's a hoax conjured up by white-collar executives in tall buildings who probably don't even ride.

At worst, it's a horrible myth that *takes* more lives than it *saves.*

The marketing slogan, popularized by loud pipes makers and one particular bike manufacturer, has spread like an invasive cancer.

If you want loud pipes because you think they sound great, that's your choice. But I'm afraid far too many riders use the concept as their first and only round of defense to lower their chances of crashing.

This makes absolutely no sense. And frankly, it's lazy.

My hunch is that most riders who subscribe to this lame hoax are likely the same ones who brag they don't use their front brake because it's dangerous and that their bike has never seen the rain.

But I can't know for sure.

The bottom line is this.
Loud pipes don't improve
your offensive or defensive
riding skills. Instead, they're
an excuse for INACTION.

With nearly half of all motorcycle crashes caused by rider error, how exactly do loud pipes help in single-vehicle accidents?

The short answer is *they don't.*

THE IDEA THAT "LOUD PIPES SAVE LIVES" IS A BAD ONE BECAUSE IT MAKES RIDERS FEEL LIKE THEY'RE DOING SOMETHING REAL TO REDUCE THEIR CHANCES OF CRASHING WHEN THEY AREN'T.

"I don't need to understand countersteering, know what low-side and high-side crashes are (and what triggers them), or wear brightly colored gear—because I have loud pipes."

Like wearing a helmet doesn't change your chances of crashing, riding a motorcycle with loud pipes doesn't keep you from crashing all by yourself—and they certainly don't help you ride better.

At best, they're hugely ineffective.

I challenge you to find the bike with loud pipes the next time you hear one while driving. I'm always amazed at how difficult they are to spot—probably because sound isn't very directional inside a car.

I've also noticed I can't hear bikes with loud pipes when the rider is approaching me in the opposite lane—where the Hurt Report showed riders were most likely to be hit by motorists turning in front of us.

The uncomfortable truth is this.

Riders would be better off with a basic knowledge of how motor-cycles work and a hi-vis yellow riding jacket.

If loud pipes saved lives, wouldn't cruiser-types crash less often? Show me that data, please. I don't think it exists.

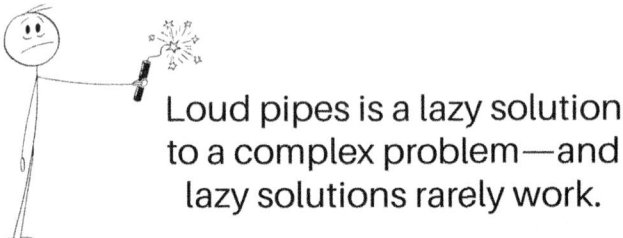

Loud pipes is a lazy solution to a complex problem—and lazy solutions rarely work.

Still not convinced? Here's what *Motorcycle Cruiser* magazine said.

Yeah, there are a few situations, like when you are right next to a driver with his window down who is about to change lanes where full-time noise-makers might help a driver notice you, but all that noise directed rearward doesn't do much in the most common and much more dangerous conflict where a car turns in front of you. Maybe it's the fatigue caused by the noise, maybe it's the attitudes of riders who insist on making annoying noise, or perhaps loud bikes annoy enough drivers to make them aggressive. Whatever the reason, the research shows that bikes with modified exhaust systems crash more frequently than those with stock pipes.[1]

What's super powerful about that statement to me is that *Cruiser* made it even though their advertising base is made up of companies that profit from the loud pipes mantra. Way to go.

SEVENTY-EIGHT

Stay Inside Your Comfort Zone

One of my mentor's best tips was to ride inside my comfort zone.

This isn't just good advice when you're riding in a group. It's good advice for when you're riding solo.

When I first started riding, I felt awkward in long sweeping curves. I rode curves slower than normal until my skills improved.

I rode at a pace that was comfortable for me.

"But Dave, how am I going to get better if I do this?"

Your comfort zone will expand with practice.

When I was struggling with curves, I found a place to practice—a cloverleaf pattern with no traffic. I studied what I was supposed to do (head knowledge), and then I practiced until my skills improved.

Riding inside your comfort zone is a good thing.

Even if that means your riding buddies
sometimes think you're pokey.

SEVENTY-NINE

Use Your Front Brake—Revisited

I told you we would come back to the topic of proper braking habits.

One of the most important reasons it's so critical to use your front brake is because your rear brake is *dangerous*. There, I said it.

As we've discussed already, a skidding rear tire is what triggers most lowside and highside crashes. But there's more.

James Davis, an expert witness in Motorcycle Dynamics, said:

> *"The most dangerous control you have on your motorcycle is your rear brake! This is because it is easy to STOP (your rear wheel) with it. […] The gyroscopic effect of a spinning rear wheel is imposed on the frame of the motorcycle and substantially determines the attitude/stability of the entire bike except for its relatively insignificant front end. To lock the rear wheel is, by definition, to remove a substantial amount of its attitude control and stability"[1]*

So, let's recap what we know about braking so far.

1. Your front brake has significantly more stopping power than your rear brake.
2. Your rear brake (without ABS) is dangerous because a locked-up rear tire can (and will) trigger a lowside or highside crash.
3. A rolling rear tire provides a huge amount of stability to your motorcycle. When you lock it up, you lose that.

Still not convinced?

Keep reading.
I'm not through with the topic.

EIGHTY

Motorcycle Crash Causation Study (MCCS)

In *Motorcycle Smarts*, I covered the Hurt Report, an extensive study on why motorcycles crash. In this chapter, I'll address a more recent study called the Motorcycle Crash Causation Study (MCCS).[1]

I just reread the 114-page MCCS Final Report for the third time, and I'm struggling with what I should say here.

Should I simply highlight some nuggets of useful information, or should I tell you what I think about the study?

I think I'll do both—but first, some background information.

The MCCS was commissioned because the number of motorcycle fatalities was going up, and our government wanted to know why.

The final report was released in 2019.

The MCCS took a much different approach than the Hurt Report. The focus for MCCS was to identify factors that contributed to crashes —hence the title "Causation."

The study looked at a large set of parameters that helped the team identify what the rider was wearing, how they might be impaired, their age, their riding experience and training, and how they crashed. To say they tracked a lot of data would be an understatement.

However, more isn't always better. I'll unpack that in a minute.

Here are seven findings I found interesting.

1. Single-vehicle crashes were overrepresented in fatal crashes.
2. Left-turn scenarios were the most common crash configuration, followed by failing to avoid a crash and running off the roadway.
3. Motorcyclists' vehicle skill deficiency contribution to crash causation contributed to the crash in 24 percent of cases and was overrepresented in single-vehicle and fatal crashes.
4. Helmets were more effective in preventing injury in multiple-vehicle crashes and less effective in reducing or preventing injury in fatal crashes.
5. Brightly colored torso garments enhanced conspicuity only in multiple-vehicle crashes.
6. Longer skid marks were overrepresented in fatal crashes for both front and rear tires.
7. Improper countersteering was overrepresented in single-vehicle crashes.

I spent a good bit of time going through the data to find the seven findings above. A large part of the findings left me underwhelmed.

Unlike the Hurt Report, which had concise takeaways, the MCCS identified each parameter as "underrepresented" or "overrepresented."

My gripe with the MCCS is that it's difficult to process.

If I handed a printed copy to 100 riders and asked them to look at it, 99 would toss it in the trash after skimming a few pages.

The one person who read it all the way through (someone like me) would read it three times (I have), figuring he was missing something. Then, if asked to list his top takeaways a week later wouldn't be able to come up with a single one (I can't).

But the thing that really upsets me about the study is the absence of some of the most important causation metrics. In other words, they neglected to properly analyze some of the most important parameters —mainly ABS, Traction Control, and Stability Control.

As you know by now, all three of these pieces of electronics 'cause' riders to crash less often by preventing most rider-induced lowside and highside crashes.

The authors included tons of parameters that can't cause anything, like whether the rider was wearing gloves. Isn't this like asking whether they were wearing boxers or briefs?

Just because you have software that can handle as many parameters as you can imagine doesn't mean you should measure all of them.

It feels like the riding community is missing the forest for the trees again. We're analyzing gobs of data in hopes of finding a smoking gun, like if riders would just wear riding gloves, they wouldn't crash.

In the end, whether you wear gloves has absolutely no causal effect on whether you crash. Neither does the color of your socks.

In contrast, the Hurt Report gives actionable steps that a rider can skim in ten minutes with meaningful takeaways.

Another one of the causations was:

"Was the rider's helmet fastened to their head?"

How can this be an indication (cause) of anything except possibly a slight leaning toward arrogance or forgetfulness?

We're missing the simple looking for the complex.

Or maybe it's we're missing the complex looking for the simple?

I couldn't help but wonder if the authors understood what triggers most *lowside* and *highside* crashes.

PERHAPS THIS BOOK SERIES SHOULD BE REQUIRED READING FOR ANYONE WORKING ON A MOTORCYCLE CRASH STUDY IN THE FUTURE.

At least then, they would understand *lowside* and *highside* crashes.

Processing through the MCCS Final Report without a consolidated list of major findings was a challenge—and poor execution.

BUT MAYBE I MISSED SOMETHING?

Just now, I went back and did a complete search for "ABS." Buried in the 114 pages of data, this is what I found:

Antilock Braking System (ABS)
'No' was overrepresented, and 'Yes' was underrepresented
in the crash data for both front and rear brakes.

That's it—all the authors had to say about something that could change the crash data. I also did a search for the following terms: *(Traction Control, Stability Control, lowside and highside crashes).* Nothing meaningful was mentioned about any of them.

I guess I'd be stating the obvious if I said
I liked the Hurt Report better.

EIGHTY-ONE

Your Favorite Bike Might Be the One You Just Sold

My mentor Fred warned me that my favorite motorcycle might be the one I had just sold. I thought that sounded odd.

It turns out that he was right—again.

It's a concept that doesn't make sense. Why would you like the motorcycle you just got rid of better than the one you just purchased?

But after you live through the experience a time or two, it actually makes perfect sense. Have you ever regretted getting rid of an old chair that fits you perfectly, even though it was worn out?

It's almost a certainty that your riding position on the motorcycle you just purchased will be different than on the one you just sold— and something is going to bother you when you first start riding it.

Maybe the riding position is more leaned forward, and your arms will be tired for carrying more weight. Maybe the foot pegs are in a different position, and your knees don't like it.

After your first long ride, there's a good chance you'll think:

I loved the motorcycle I just sold.

The bike I missed the most after I sold it was my Honda VFR. It was my first real motorcycle. Passing was a rush of adrenaline. It wasn't the fastest one out there, but it *was* the fastest one I've ever owned.

EIGHTY-TWO

What Makes a Rider Good?

Saying you're a great rider because you're good at low-speed control is like saying you're a great basketball player because you can dribble.

It doesn't work that way.

When I was in the 7th grade, I tried out for the basketball team.

When I compared myself to the other boys there, I felt confident I would make the team because I was the best one there at free throws.

I was devastated when the coaches told me I didn't.

The players who ended up making the team were good at shooting, dribbling, rebounding, *and* playing defense. I was good at shooting.

It took me years to gain the wisdom that being good at shooting free throws didn't mean I was good at playing basketball.

It's the same with motorcycles. Being good at low-speed maneuvers doesn't make you a good rider. You might be able to make your motorcycle go around tight cones and still not understand that you should use your front brake—or that locking up your rear tire is what triggers most lowside and highside crashes.

Being great at basketball takes more than shooting free throws.

Riding to Alaska without crashing means nothing.

Nor does completing an Iron Butt (or two) or deciding to wear a full face helmet and ride a bike with loud pipes.

There's more to being a good rider than that.

Being a good rider starts with the mindset of becoming an even better rider. It almost always encompasses a willingness to be different than your buddies and to learn everything you can about the sport.

I'm not saying being good at low-speed control is a waste of time.

I'm simply making the point that it takes a suite of tools to become a great rider. In the 7th grade, I was good at shooting free throws.

Looking back, I now understand why that wasn't enough.

BECOMING A PROFICIENT RIDER STARTS WITH MINDSET, BUILDS WITH HEAD KNOWLEDGE, AND FINISHES WITH SOLID EXECUTION.

All this fits together like a glove.

I keep remembering what Hurt said in an interview years after the Hurt Report was published—that even the most highly trained police motorcycle officers (no doubt great at low-speed control) oftentimes made the same mistakes as novices—including overusing (locking up) their rear tire in emergency stops.[1]

Sometimes, I think we're missing the forest for the trees
when it comes to rider education.

EIGHTY-THREE

Do Something—Anything to Avoid a Crash

The data is overwhelming. Every motorcycle crash study I've seen—including the Hurt Report, MCCS, and others—has shown that riders oftentimes don't do *anything* to avoid an imminent crash.

Hurt found that riders didn't make the *correct* evasive maneuver to avoid crashing in most situations. Even worse, his research showed that riders didn't attempt *any* evasive maneuver 32 percent of the time.[1]

How can this be true?

When my kids started driving, I told them that someday they might have to decide between two bad outcomes—and that their *best* option might be to avoid the *worst* option.

Run into a ditch or hit a pedestrian? Take the ditch.

Hit a dog or a bicyclist? Take out the dog.

Hit a car or run off the road? Run off the road.

My point in having this discussion was to help them think ahead and realize that neither of the options before you might be good, but that you should still decide which is worse and avoid that one.

The same holds true when you're riding a motorcycle.

When things go bad, every rider needs to do whatever is necessary to avoid the worst outcome.

This might mean you maneuver your bike into a field instead of hitting a car head-on. It might mean that you brake as hard as you can to reduce your speed before you hit the thing in front of you. It might mean that you hit a curb instead of the kid crossing the road.

But it might also mean that you swerve (using countersteering) to avoid the thing you're about to hit if you don't do *something*.

The takeaway from the crash studies is crystal clear.

A large percentage of riders who are about to hit something don't do ANYTHING to avoid hitting the thing they're about to hit. NOTHING!

The first line of defense to avoiding a crash is understanding countersteering and braking—with your head. Read *Motorcycle Smarts.*

You can make your motorcycle do crazy things by pushing on the handlebars. You can also stop on a dime if you use your front brake and have ABS and Traction Control.

My challenge to everyone (me included) is to prepare mentally that someday you might need to do an evasive maneuver to avoid a crash.

Commit to yourself that you will do *something* and select the best option even when none of the options before you are ideal.

All this starts with *head knowledge.*

It springs into action with *muscle memory.*

And it's finished with solid *execution.*

If you do SOMETHING (anything) to avoid an imminent crash, that means you're doing more than a lot of riders. I know—crazy.

EIGHTY-FOUR

A Fresh Approach: Part Two

Riders are crashing in single-vehicle crashes (all by ourselves) at the same rate we did generations ago. Why is this acceptable?

We have mandatory training requirements, more skills books, and more crash data than ever before—yet nothing is getting better.

Something needs to change.

Why don't *all* riders with training know what triggers most lowside and highside crashes? Why is there so much hate for ABS?

Why isn't the crash data showing improvements? The only logical conclusion is that the training isn't working.

We're also missing the mark on motorcycle causation studies.

Whether your passenger was wearing gloves has nothing to do with whether you understand how to ride a motorcycle, and it certainly isn't a good indicator of how likely you are to crash.

I took another look at the Motorcycle Causation Crash Study and found that it hardly mentioned ABS.[1] Why is this? Was it too hard? How can it be that one of the most powerful aids to keep riders from triggering single-vehicle crashes was left off the list of things to study?

We can do better than this. We must do better than this.

We need studies with a wider geographical footprint and narrower list of causation parameters. We need to figure a way to simplify things we're measuring so a police report and interview with the crash victims (if they survived) would suffice.

But Universities won't get rich with simple studies. Right?

More data isn't always better information. Instead, let's test some of the heavy hitters I've addressed in the *Motorcycle Smarts* book series. We deserve to know the truth.

Riders need to know if bikes with ABS, ESC, and Traction Control crash less often (or more often) than ones with regular brakes.

Riders need to know if loud pipes save lives—because if they don't, we're doing folks a huge disservice by not telling them the truth.

Riders need to know what segment of riders crash the most because once we know this, we can focus more attention on educating them.

 Most studies try to determine what riders who crash are doing. I want to know what riders who DON'T crash are doing.

What do they wear?

How did they learn how to ride?

Do they ride motorcycles with ABS and Traction Control?

How many miles do they ride every year?

What color is their riding gear?

Sure, this type of study might take more thought and execution, but it might simply involve a questionnaire—much easier to administer than onsite crash analysis.

And we snub our nose at the Hurt Report from the 80s like it was done by cavemen. Give me a freaking break.

ANYWAY YOU SLICE IT, THE HURT REPORT GIVES RIDERS REAL DATA ON HOW WE TEND TO CRASH. WHAT WE DO WITH IT IS UP TO US.

It doesn't really take a rocket scientist to figure all this out.

Riders crash and die every day because they went wide in a turn.

Riders crash and die every day because they locked up their rear tire and lowsided or highsided.

Riders crash and die every day because motorists didn't see them.

Riders crash and die every day because they refuse to use their front brake enough—probably because someone told them they'd be catapulted over their handlebars—even though this is never the case with normal motorcycles, and every motorcycle instructor knows it.

Were the instructors too busy talking about selecting a helmet to mention this in hands-on training?

I'm afraid there are a few low-information riders who still believe using your front brake is bad—and a high portion of them ride cruisers. Just an educated hunch based on personal observations.

In large part, we (the riding community) are killing ourselves.

SOMETHING'S NOT WORKING.

We need to look at the way we're training beginning riders because the data suggests we need a different approach.

We need to educate all riders on lowside and highside crashes and what causes them.

We need ABS, ESC, and Traction Control on all street bikes.

And last but not least, we need congress to mandate ABS (then traction Control and ESC) on all street motorcycles sold in the U.S.

If this book series makes that happen one day sooner, this journey has been more than worth it.

WE CAN DO THIS IF WE WORK TOGETHER!

And the first step in this process is to admit there's a problem.

———————

Hey. Real quick.

*Have you signed up for the 'Motorcycle Smarts' Quick Tips
Newsletter yet? It's where I share some of my best riding tips,
(some of which didn't make it into any of my books).
They're simple. They're powerful. They're free.
Sign up at the link below. Unsubscribe at any time.*

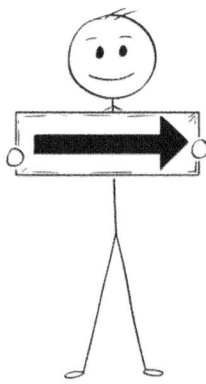

"Motorcycle Smarts" Quick Tips Newsletter

Free weekly riding tips you can
consume in less than 3 minutes—
delivered to your inbox for you to use
and share with others.

motorcyclesmarts.com/tips

You're not doing everything you can to keep from crashing until you're signed up.

———————

motorcyclesmarts.com/tips

EIGHTY-FIVE

Intersections

Intersections are rough on riders.

After rereading some of the crash data in preparation for this book, intersections are even worse than I remembered.

The statistics between studies vary slightly, but it's probably safe to say that roughly half of all *crashes* occur in intersections, and one-third of all motorcycle *fatalities* occur in intersections.

As I've said before, recognizing this information (head knowledge) is the first step in reducing the chances you'll crash.

I wish I had a tip to keep you safe in all intersections, but I don't.

Unless you're a superhero, avoiding them isn't an option either.

So what *can* you do to decrease your risks? Aside from the obvious: ride defensively, look for distracted drivers around you, and be visible, there are a few extra things you can do.

I'll share those next.

EIGHTY-SIX

Wait Three Seconds

Now that we've determined that intersections are dangerous for riders, let's talk about something you can do to lower your risks.

The worst position waiting at a traffic signal is the first in line. This is because you'll be the first one in the intersection when it turns green. If someone runs a red light, you'll be the one they hit.

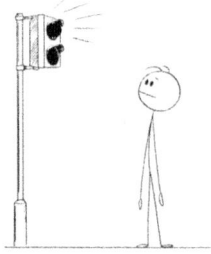

When I'm the first one in line at the light, I always wait three seconds after the light turns green before I go.

Obviously, I look first, but adding this pause gives folks in a hurry a few seconds of margin to run the red light.

"But Dave, don't drivers behind you get upset?"

I've noticed over time that drivers behind me only get frustrated if they don't think I saw the light had turned green. As long as I begin to make some form of motion—pulling in clutch, putting in gear, and looking like I'm about to take off—they never honk at me.

Three seconds isn't all that long.

I also do this when I'm driving. I usually take my foot off the brake so my brake light will go off. This lets folks know I saw the light.

Want to reduce your chances of crashing in an intersection?

*Wait three seconds after the
light turns green before you proceed.*

EIGHTY-SEVEN

Car Blockers

Following up on our discussion on intersections, there's something else you can do to reduce your chances of crashing going through them.

The crash studies have shown that a large percentage of motorists who failed to yield to riders in intersections said that they didn't see us.

Even when we wear bright gear, we're sometimes hard to spot.

When I ride through intersections, I try to find a car nearby that I can ride close to and use as my car blocker.

I put myself in a position that keeps me safe as long as drivers see and avoid my car blocker. This might mean that I get *behind* my car blocker when I'm approaching a normal intersection or possibly *next* to my car blocker when I go through a four-lane intersection.

Every situation is different.

As long as others can see my car blocker, I'm a little safer.

CAR BLOCKERS AREN'T JUST GOOD IN INTERSECTIONS.

I'm always looking for car blockers, especially in congested areas.

Just be careful not to ride in your car blocker's blind spot for long. This usually seems like a good spot, but it creates risks of its own.

Before we leave this topic, let me say this.

NOTE: It's important to note that when you're using a car blocker, you're not making it more likely *they'll* crash. You're just making it less likely that *you* will.

Want to change your chances of crashing?

Find a car blocker and tag along.

EIGHTY-EIGHT

My Problem With Trickle Chargers

What I'm about to say is going to ruffle some feathers.

I'm not a huge fan of battery trickle chargers.

I know the manufacturers taunt the advantages, but the disadvantages really mess with my mojo. There, I said it.

Case in point.

When I leave for a long ride, I want to know the true condition of my battery. If it's been plugged into a trickle charger, I'm not going to know that until I'm days from home.

But if I let the alternator and battery do their normal thing with normal riding, if my battery seems in good condition when I leave, it's likely going to be in good condition weeks later.

Just so you know, I'm also a battery snob on my cell phone. I don't care what the "experts" say. I always totally discharge (and fully charge) my cell phone every single time. While this isn't a statistically significant event, my cell phone, that's six years old, holds a longer charge than everyone in my family who has much newer phones.

My friends in colder climates say I'm nuts—and maybe they're right. I'm just saying that trickle chargers disguise real problems.

That makes *me* not interested.

EIGHTY-NINE

Calling It Quits

The idea of calling it quits is a topic that's close to my heart. I've been listening for the muse to call my name for years.

If I listen closely, I hear its faint voice in the distance.

"Dave, it's time to pick a different craft."

I think most riders will eventually hear the same voice.

Several years ago, this voice called out to my mentor, Fred—in part because he was wise enough to listen out for it.

Fred was always looking for signs it might be time to stop riding. He got the sign one afternoon while driving with his wife.

He was on unfamiliar roads and barreled through a four-way stop without even noticing it. The stop sign wasn't in a low-traffic neighborhood. It was on a pretty significant highway.

"David, I could have killed someone.

"Maybe this is my sign that I should stop riding a motorcycle."

Fred was wise enough to look for warning signs. And he was also wise enough to do something when they showed up.

A short time later, Fred sold his motorcycle. It was a difficult decision for him. Fred had been riding since he was a kid.

He was sad when he told me—but excited too.

"David, I've gotten a lot of enjoyment out of riding motorcycles, but I think it's time to do something else. It's been a good ride."

This lesson from Fred was perhaps his greatest as my mentor.

Fred didn't just tell me. He *showed* me that it's okay to stop riding a motorcycle when the pleasures of riding no longer trump the risks.

I respected his decision. I know it wasn't an easy one to make.

How Old Is Too Old?

I would never suggest a particular age as being too old to ride a motorcycle. I know riders who have all the physical and mental abilities to do just fine who are much older than I am.

But that doesn't mean I shouldn't stop riding before they do.

And there's no magical age that you should start looking for signs. But fifty is probably a good time to start making yearly assessments of your riding skills and whether you should continue for another year.

I want to stop riding on my terms, not when life decides for me.

And I won't let pride or stubbornness stand in my way.

WHEN MY SOUL WHISPERS THAT IT'S TIME TO STOP RIDING, I'LL LISTEN—AND I'LL STOP!

———

I hope you will too.

NINETY

Ride to Nowhere

Some of my most enjoyable rides have been on the way to nowhere.

One time I headed out on a beautiful fall morning and purposefully didn't carry a map. At each intersection, I made the real-time call whether to turn right, turn left, or go straight.

It was amazing.

Another time I rode north from home and found an old country store that reminded me of a place when I was a kid.

Rides to nowhere don't have rules or timelines. You're allowed to discover things at a pace that works best for you.

And the silent thoughts in my helmet
are sometimes the best part.

NINETY-ONE

Riding in the Rain—Part 2

I think some riders have the misconception that getting caught on a motorcycle in the rain is somehow a failure.

That's not the case at all.

It just means you're not afraid of getting wet.

If you've never ridden in the rain, a good place to start is near your house. That's what Fred suggested when I bought my first motorcycle.

"Dave, you should take your motorcycle out sometime when it's raining so you can see what it's like. You can stay close to home and wander back if you run into any real problems."

This is one of the rare times that I didn't follow Fred's advice. But I should have. I would have known what to expect that day.

Instead, I relied on a weatherman to keep me dry.

That didn't work out so well.

I'll share that story a little later.

NINETY-TWO

Wear a Helmet—If You Want

Whether you wear a helmet when you ride is your choice—at least in states without mandatory helmet laws.

Readers are usually surprised about my stance on this.

If I were to obsess about my preference to wear a full face helmet, I think it would take away from other topics I'm passionate about.

In other words, some would ignore *everything* I had to say because they didn't like me preaching to them about helmets.

It's not my purpose to change anyone's mind about helmets.

My passion is to help riders keep from crashing.

For the same reason that arguing shorter stopping distances is the main reason for ABS is faulty, arguing the solution to reducing motorcycle fatalities is helmet usage misses the mark too.

Don't mistake wearing a helmet as a means to reduce your chances of crashing. They don't. They just reduce your chances of a head injury (or death) if you do crash.

Riders wearing even the best helmets crash and die every day in single-vehicle crashes all by themselves—caused by rider error.

Helmets don't fix our
failure to educate riders,
and they're the last thing
we should count on to
keep us alive.

When I started riding, I *wanted* to wear a full face helmet, but I wasn't sure I could. I don't like confined spaces.

Fortunately, I was able to get used to it pretty fast.

Now, I find that riding with a full face helmet is more comfortable because it keeps air away from my face and eyes.

They're great when it's cold and wet too.

When vacationing in Florida every year (no helmet laws), I rarely see someone in a group who isn't following the norm of the group.

Either *all* the riders in the group are wearing helmets—or *none* of them are. I find that troubling. Is peer pressure still a thing?

If you're on the fence about helmets, here's something interesting from an NHTSA study. I especially like the last sentence.

> *"Helmets are estimated to be 37 percent effective in preventing fatal injuries to motorcycle riders and 41 percent for motorcycle passengers. In other words, for every 100 motorcycle riders killed in crashes while not wearing helmets, 37 of them could have been saved had all 100 worn helmets."*

NINETY-THREE

Cancel Your Turn Signal

There's nothing more distracting than riding behind your riding buddy with his turn signal blinking endlessly.

Not only is this distracting, but it's also dangerous.

The conversation was always awkward.

"Mike, You're probably better off not using your turn signals if you can't remember to cancel them."

Years later, helmet communications fixed this. I simply talk in my helmet, and he hears me. "Mike, your turn signal is still on."

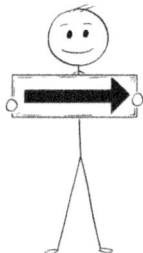

Signaling to motorists
where you're going and
then NOT going there
seems more dangerous
than NOT signaling at all.

NINETY-FOUR

Cautiously Participate Online

The internet is a wonderful thing. But be careful.

Just because somebody said it doesn't make it fact.

When I started riding, I went online for advice. Later, I discovered that a lot of what I found was wrong.

How do you know if what you're reading is accurate?

You don't. Forums can be the worst—and the topic of brakes is at the top of the list of things that gets butchered.

Unfortunately, the loudest voices are often the most incorrect.

Several years back, a frustrated *Motorcycle Mentor Podcast* listener emailed me for help. He had read in one forum that you should never use your *front* brake and in another forum that you should never use your *rear* brake. His last words were, "Please help!"

Forums are fun, but
they're not always
the best source of
information.

It's better to stick with well-known sources for things that matter.

In the first draft of this book, I included several forum posts with incorrect advice to show you how crazy they were. I decided to delete them because I didn't want to present the wrong information here.

The Internet is a wonderful thing
—when used properly.

NINETY-FIVE

Prepare an Emergency
Contact Information Sheet

No rider wants to think about it. But every rider should plan for it.

One of the kindest (most thoughtful) things you can do for your riding buddies is to make an Emergency Contact information sheet.

I keep mine in my tank bag on a 3x5 orange index card.

Then, when I ride in a group, I simply tell someone:

"Hey, there's an orange index card in my tank bag
that has my wife's contact information."

Sure, it's usually an awkward moment—but that's fine.

Before Mike and I rode to Alaska, I asked him to send me his wife Michelle's number. He rolled his eyes at me. I didn't care.

Then, I told him I was sending him Sue's.

And he rolled his eyes—again.

NINETY-SIX

Riding in Groups: Choose Wisely

Randy might be a great poker buddy, but are you sure you want to ride a motorcycle close to him?

Would you let Randy borrow your brand new $60k sports car?

Does Randy favor his rear brake?

Choosing who you ride with is way more important than choosing who you trust to drive your car.

Think of it this way. If the rider behind you only uses their rear brake, and you make an emergency stop using your front brake, they'll crash into you because you'll stop more quickly than them.

Does Randy understand lowside and highside crashes and what triggers them? Does Randy have a temper? Does Randy wear gear that makes him difficult to see?

Riders crash and die every day because they chose the wrong folks to ride with.

Who we ride with matters.

NINETY-SEVEN

A Restroom Hand Dryer

Hand dryers in restrooms aren't just for hands.

The first time I had the idea was somewhere in Kentucky.

Mike had purchased a motorcycle in Indianapolis. He flew up to get it, and I met him halfway back in Elizabethtown, Kentucky.

That was my first long ride by myself. It was magical.

On the ride back the next day, we ran into rain. Neither of us had good rain gear—and we were wet, cold, and miserable.

We stopped at a fast food place for refuge and to use the restroom. Partway through my bathroom break, I glanced over and noticed the hand dryer mounted on the wall.

At first, I figured I'd just enjoy the warmth of the heat on my cold hands. Seconds later, I realized I could use it to dry my gloves.

It worked like a charm.

NINETY-EIGHT

Represent the Sport

When you ride a motorcycle, what you do is a reflection on me—and what I do when I ride is a reflection on you.

There's really no way around that.

When you blare your stereo at the light, cut a motorist off because they made an error, or lose your cool because someone pulled out in front of you, drivers think I'm like you when they see me.

And just so you know, when you crank up your stereo at a traffic light, you look like a seventeen-year-old showing off his new Kenwood stereo from Walmart.

Do you realize everyone is laughing at you when you do this?

The same goes for blipping your throttle to show off your pipes—annoying, childish, and embarrassing to the entire riding community.

My favorite (sarcasm) is when I go to the beach during bike week to write and without fail a group of riders, no doubt returning from a wet tee-shirt contest, pulls in and revs their engines at 3 a.m.

Is this really necessary?

Does anyone with a brain think this is cool?

The frustrating thing is that the people you woke up blaring your music at 3 a.m. assume that I'm just like you when they see me.

I know what some of you are thinking:

"I ride a Harley and don't blare my stereo or blip my throttle."

And that's exactly the point I'm trying to make!

What a few do is a reflection on all of us—including you.

This sort of childish behavior by a few riders gives all riders a bad reputation.
And that's NOT RIGHT!

Can you sense my frustration?

Truth be told, I think Harley Davidson should have to pay a fine for every bike they make with a mega-stereo in the dash. Put a drunk guy who thinks he looks badass on a bike with a big stereo—and you'll end up with classic rock from the 80s at 120 dB every time.

A quick question for the folks who do this:

Do you think it's cool when someone pulls up for gas and leaves their stereo blaring while they go inside? I didn't think so.

All I'm suggesting is basic courtesy. Let the guy ahead of you merge into traffic. Wave to the toddler in the car next to you.

And smile!

NINETY-NINE

Take Every Ride Seriously

Every ride has the potential to teach you something.

Every ride has the potential to be your last.

I keep a pen and paper in my tank bag. When I have an idea about something I need to improve, I write myself a note at the next stop.

My wife says I have a short-term memory problem and that I take so many notes because of it. Honestly, I don't remember if that's true.

She also says I'm not very logical—which honestly makes me question her stance on my short-term memory problem.

My riding notes might look something like this:

"I used my rear brake waytoo much when I was cruising around in the neighborhood. Stop David! How you ride putzing about defines what you'll do in an emergency situation."

EVERY RIDE HAS THE POTENTIAL TO TEACH US SOMETHING. BUT ONLY IF WE'RE WILLING TO LISTEN AND TAKE NOTES.

ONE HUNDRED

Ride Reports

I kept a journal during my first year by emailing my mentor Fred.

We called them *ride reports*. I think Fred enjoyed reading them as much as I enjoyed writing them because they took him back to when he first started riding—which was a very long time ago.

Looking back, I think Fred was *making* me keep a journal without *telling* me to keep a journal. Thanks, Fred.

Your first year on a bike will be a journey you don't want to forget.

You'll notice new sights and smells on the same roads you've traveled hundreds of times before. You'll experience the awesomeness of a Saturday morning ride to nowhere.

Sometimes it's hard for me to remember the awe of that first year.

Keeping a journal isn't just for beginners. It's for anyone who will pause for long enough to capture the moment in the present.

Taking a Break Is Normal

"Ten days after my friend bought his first motorcycle, he was in an accident. Days later, he was declared brain dead."—via email

The data doesn't lie. Riding a motorcycle is riskier than riding in a car.

The reason I'm making this point is that we must all constantly weigh the risks of riding during each stage in life.

It might make sense for you to ride now, and not make sense when you have two toddlers at home.

Don't miss my point here. I'm not saying we shouldn't ride when we have young kids. I'm saying that from the emails I've received that it's perfectly normal to pause from riding at different stages in life.

Ride for a few years because the risks are manageable.

Pause for a few years because the risks are too great.

A trend I've noticed over the years is that guys who rode when they were younger (and stopped) decide to give it a shot later in life.

There's nothing wrong with that, either.

Others simply stop riding when the enjoyment factor dissipates. In either case, riding a motorcycle during certain periods in your life and *not* riding during other periods is perfectly normal—and healthy.

When the pleasures of riding don't offset the risks, stop or pause. Your riding buddies will understand.

If they don't, find some real friends.

Use Your Front Brake—A Thinking Exercise

What I'm about to say might strike a nerve in some.

You might want to go ahead and sit down.

Removing the rear brake on all normal motorcycles (designed by engineers for on-street use) would, perhaps, change the crash data more than any other single thing we could do because it would force riders to use their front brake. It would also eliminate some of the most common rider-induced crashes.

It would save lives! Crazy, I know.

Obviously, I can't be an advocate for this since adding a little rear brake to your front brake squeeze in a panic stop will likely stop you a tad quicker. But it's still worth considering.

I make this point to illustrate the thrust of what I'm talking about —and to help riders who are still on the fence about using their front brake to ponder the idea.

It's a valid point. Maybe I should take up the cause?

On second thought …

WHY SHOULD I HAVE TO GIVE UP MY REAR BRAKE FOR RIDERS WHO ARE TOO STUBBORN TO LEARN/KNOW/ACCEPT THAT AVOIDING YOUR FRONT BRAKE IS CRAZY?

Answer: I shouldn't.

ONE HUNDRED THREE

Ride With Margin

From a physics perspective, motorcycles are simply amazing.

That's one of the things that draws me toward them. It's also why I've spent so much time studying how they work and why they crash.

At any given moment, there are only a few square inches of rubber in contact with the asphalt.

Margin is the difference between the limits of your tires and what you're asking them to do in that instant. Margin is the thing you can call on if the driver coming your way pulls in front of you.

Margin is that little extra you can call on in a pinch.

Closed-off Moto GP tracks are perfectly maintained, and the rider who rides with the *least* amount of margin in the race usually wins.

Normal riding isn't like that.

Margin is what I needed in a curve laced with gravel. Margin is what I needed when a car pulled out in front of me just the other day.

Margin is your best friend on a motorcycle. And riders who ride with it usually outlive their riding buddies who don't.

Wait Thirty Minutes

I'm sure you know this already, but I thought I would say it again.

It's better *not to ride* for thirty minutes after it starts raining.

Vehicles drop oil and other fluids that seep into the asphalt. When it rains, these fluids come back up to the surface.

It usually takes about thirty minutes for the rain to wash it away.

Run over a slick spot under heavy throttle, and you'll be on the ground wondering what-the-heck-just-happened before you know it.

Well, that is unless you have Traction Control or Stability Control.

The workaround is simple. Just don't ride for thirty minutes.

Use common sense. If it rained yesterday, you're probably fine to ride sooner. If it hasn't rained in months, you should wait even longer.

My Dad used to say, "Nothing good happens after midnight."

He was right. Along those lines, I'll make this point.

"Nothing good happens on a motorcycle for the first thirty minutes after it starts raining."

Disconnect from Technology

When I bought my first bike, paper maps still existed. Part of the joy of riding for me was getting away from the noise of my normal life.

I got lost more than once, and I enjoyed every minute.

Years later, after GPS was common, I still took rides with it turned off so I could feel the uncomfortableness of not knowing where I was.

When was the last time you didn't know where you were?

Those are the magical moments that I still remember.

If you're like most people, one of the first things you'll want to do after you buy your first motorcycle is to purchase a GPS navigation system—connected via Bluetooth to your smartphone—which is then connected wirelessly to your helmet speaker system.

If you do this, you'll be missing out on one of the most incredible experiences you'll ever encounter in your life—riding a motorcycle in the solitude of Mother Nature.

Do you really want to miss out on this?

Without technology to help, I've been lost ten miles from home.

I still remember the incredible sensation—and the freedom.

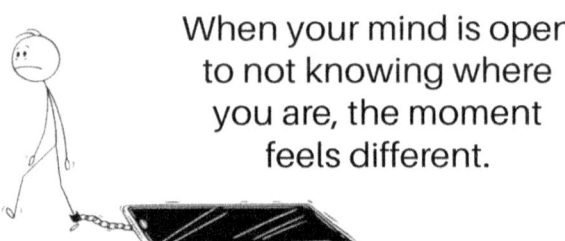

When your mind is open
to not knowing where
you are, the moment
feels different.

And then, someday, you can get tired of the unknown and add all the gadgets your heart desires.

Instead of focusing on how to operate your new GPS, experience the freedom of not knowing where you are.

Instead of listening to your favorite music track, notice the sounds and smells of Mother Nature around you.

Instead of checking where you are, focus on where you want to go.

Don't get me wrong. There's a time and a place for gadgets. I have plenty of them in my life. But one of the most amazing parts of riding a motorcycle is disconnecting from those distractions.

At least once in a while.

Make Sure You're In First Gear

One of the most dangerous things we do is go across lanes of traffic.

The mental habit of MAKING SURE you're in first gear is the first step in any successful launch. It's even more important to check and double-check when you might get run over if you stall.

It's the same thing in an automobile with a manual transmission.

If your motorcycle has an indicator that signals what gear you're in, it's also a good habit to glance down and triple-check.

One thing I like to do when possible is to launch the motorcycle and get out of the friction zone *before* I initiate a left turn across traffic. I do the same thing in a car with a manual.

I also bump up the RPMs higher than normal.

Nobody is grading your launch here. Making it across the lanes of oncoming traffic successfully is the only thing that counts.

And that all begins with making
sure you're in first gear.

Don't Ignore the Warning Signs

Crashes and dropped bikes are warning signs—even if they're minor.

I'm not suggesting you stop riding if you drop your motorcycle in your driveway or veer into a ditch, but I have seen riders laugh at both as though they're normal—and they're not.

Instead, I think all mishaps are signs that your skills aren't where they should be. Why did you drop your motorcycle? Did you forget to put your feet down? Is your bike too big? What about the crash? Were you riding outside your comfort zone? Was it your fault?

Here's what Marty wrote:

"I just started riding two months ago. I passed my training class with ease. Two weeks later, I skidded out in a curve and crashed. Then two weeks ago, while taking a corner at ten mph, I became mesmerized by a fire hydrant. I crashed right into it and broke my wrist. My first thought was that I had no business thinking I could learn to ride at 59. Weeks later, I now see both incidents as normal beginner mistakes."

WHAT DO YOU THINK MARTY SHOULD DO? SHOULD HE BLOW OFF THESE CRASHES AS NORMAL BEGINNER MISTAKES?

I'll say this again. I believe riding should begin with *head knowledge*.

In Marty's case, he ran into the fire hydrant because that's where he was looking. Remember the discussion earlier about *target fixation*?

And why did he lowside in the curve? Did he lock up his rear tire? Did he have ABS or Traction Control?

Warning signs are clues, and they should never be ignored.

Listen carefully.

A Few Feet Away From Death

Every second we're on a motorcycle, we're feet away from death.

I know this sounds morbid, but I think it's important to realize. What might be a minor fender bender if you run into a curb in your car might look like death if you bump into it on your motorcycle.

If you run wide by a foot on a mountainous road in a car, you still have two tires on solid ground. If you run wide in the same curve on a motorcycle, you're going to crash.

The more miles I ride, the more powerful this awareness becomes.

I saw this firsthand once when a riding buddy ran over a patch of gravel in a curve. He crashed instantly. If he had been in an automobile, he would have hardly noticed a thing.

During our ride back from Alaska, I'll never forget what the attendant at an old country store told us when Mike and I stopped for gas right before we rode the *Million Dollar Highway*.

"PLEASE BE CAREFUL. RIDERS CRASH AND DIE EVERY WEEK ON THE STRETCH OF ROAD YOU GUYS ARE ABOUT TO RIDE."

I'm almost certain she didn't say that to her customers in cars.

I sensed that she was silently processing what it might feel like if it was one of us who was next—like riders she had told the same thing to before that didn't make it to the other side of the mountain.

Seven years later, I can still hear her voice inside my helmet.

"Riders crash and die on the road you guys are about to ride."

And I like it that she's still in there with me.

Who Needs Shelter?

When I first started riding, I thought I needed to find shelter when it started raining. Now I think that's funny.

Back in the day, I wrote an article that listed my favorite spots: gas stations, bank drive-throughs, school and church drop-offs, car washes, and underpasses. That was a lot of miles ago.

I suppose a shelter might be good for when you get caught without gear because the weatherman said there was a zero chance of rain.

That happened to me once.

Now I take rain gear with me everywhere I go.

During a recent ride to New York state, Mike and I got caught in a winter storm. It was miserable outside in the low 40s and raining when we loaded our bikes in the early morning in Paint Bank, Virginia.

I silently wished my GS wouldn't start.

That's when I realized that *touring* on a motorcycle is different.

When you're starting and ending points are the same for your ride, the weather might matter. But when you're trying to get to somewhere before sundown, it doesn't so much.

When you're on a ride far
from home, you put on the
best gear that you have
—and you keep going.

No excuses. No stories. No option to wait for better weather.

Mike and I were miserable, but neither of us said a thing because we knew that staying in the comfort of indoor heat wasn't an option.

At that moment, I realized why riding a motorcycle to somewhere far away can be so magical—and that the uncomfortable morning cold and rain was one of the reasons why.

To be fully immersed in Mother Nature is one of the most amazing parts of any adventure on two wheels.

ONE HUNDRED TEN

Riding Curves a Different Way

I'm apprehensive about what I'm about to suggest because it's counter to everything that's been written about the topic.

When I started riding, curves gave me fits.

Everything got better once I started keeping my head level with the ground (see Chapter 20), but sometimes I still get disoriented.

Just ask Mike how far ahead he gets when we ride twisty roads. Sometimes I think it annoys him. But that's what friends are for, right?

He likes curves more than straight roads and rides them fast.

I like straight roads just fine and ride curves not as fast.

Which leads me to my thoughts about riding curves.

All the books and training I've seen all agree that the correct way to ride through a curve on a motorcycle is to enter the curve toward the *outside* line and countersteer your way through.

See Figures 110-1 and 110-2 (below).

I agree this is the best way to ride through a curve: better visibility around the curve, and less friction required from your tires because the radius of the arc you're riding isn't as sharp.

But here's my issue with this.

It's easy for riders to get this backward and instead enter the curve on the *inside* line—which is the worst way to ride a curve.

Riding the curve from this entry point is actually dangerous.

See Figures 110-1 and 110-2 (below).

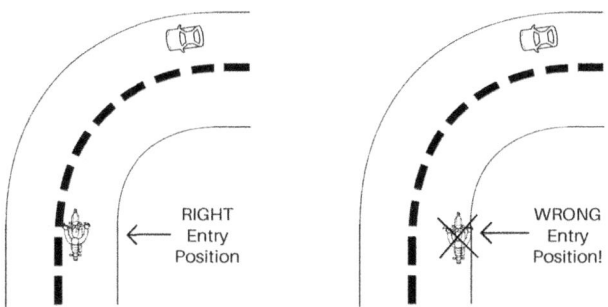

Figure 110-1 Entry Position for Curve to the Right

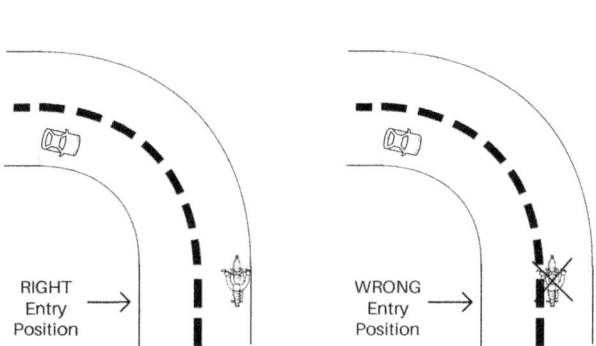

Figure 110-2 Entry Position for Curve to the Left

I've seen hundreds of crashes on YouTube where the rider entered the curve on the *inside* line and couldn't make the curve and crashed.

Listen. I'm not judging riders for making this mistake. I've made it tons of times even though I know where I'm supposed to enter.

So, what am I suggesting?

THE SECOND BEST WAY TO RIDE A CURVE ISN'T THE BEST WAY, BUT IT ISN'T THE WORST WAY–WHICH WE'VE DETERMINED IS DANGEROUS.

The second best way to ride a curve is to follow the curve of the road. Simply staying in the middle of your lane is probably the simplest.

The naysayers will point out (correctly) that there's a higher chance for road grime dropped from cars in the middle of the lane.

But I'd counter that by pointing out that even if you take the best line, you're still riding in the middle of your lane during parts of it.

DON'T GET ME WRONG. I'M NOT SUGGESTING YOU RIDE A CURVE THIS WAY EVERY TIME.

What I am suggesting is that *if* you find yourself riding the worst line (which is dangerous), you might be better off riding down the middle of your lane until you get everything sorted out and corrected.

I'll take it a step further.

I've looked at the geometry around the popular claim that entering a curve on the *outside* gives you better visibility—and it's *insignificant*.

We're talking a fraction of a second that you might be able to see a hazard more quickly. I could make the claim that riding so close to the edge of the road (outside line in a left-handed curve) is riskier.

I'll spare you from the exact calculations, but I estimate at 40 mph (59 ft/sec) going around a curve in the *best* line could potentially allow you to see a perfectly placed hazard around the curve .25 seconds faster than if you were in the *middle* of your lane. Hardly worth the risk.

Of course, the angle of the curve and your speed affects this.

This increased visibility argument has been repeated so many times that folks think it's true. And no one challenged it—until now.

So, with the visibility advantage debunked, we're left with the only reason to ride the *best* line in a curve is to ask less from your tires. But wouldn't it be the same if you just did curves with *margin*?

WAIT! I NEED TO MAKE THE FOLLOWING POINT ONCE MORE.

When you make a mistake and enter a left-handed curve near the left part of your lane or a right-handed curve on the right part of your lane —both WRONG (the worst)—you'll have to ask more from your tires than if you were riding the natural arc of the curve.

Are you at least following my train of thought here?

Remember when I made the claim that removing the rear brake on all street motorcycles would likely decrease the number of fatalities?

Well, here's another claim to make you think.

I don't have scientific data to support this, but I bet fewer riders would crash in curves if all riders followed the arc of the curve.

I'm not advocating either.

I'm just making a point for you to consider.

IF YOU'RE UNSURE OR GET CONFUSED WHEN ENTERING A CURVE, CONSIDER ENTERING THE CURVE IN THE MIDDLE OF YOUR LANE AND FOLLOWING THE ARC OF THE CURVE–BECAUSE THAT'S NOT AS DANGEROUS AS ENTERING THE CURVE IN THE WRONG POSITION.

I'm sure you know this already, but if a Moto GP racer didn't take the best (correct) line in every curve, he'd be in last place in every race.

But that's not our goal. It's for fewer riders to crash in curves.

I'm glad I decided to include this chapter. It's never easy to present an idea that goes counter to what's accepted as common and correct.

Riding In Groups: The Best Position

I have one last thing to say about riding in groups.

When you're riding in a group, consider riding in the back.

My mentor Fred thought riding in the back was the safest spot. It's definitely my favorite position.

One of the biggest reasons I like it back there is that I don't have to think about folks watching me ride. I know that sounds silly, but it's distracting to me nonetheless.

And being distracted isn't a good thing on a motorcycle.

Another thing I like about riding in the back is that no one gets separated except me if I lose the rider ahead of me.

And when I'm in the back, I can also go slower around things I want and then catch back up. When folks are behind me, I feel pressure to ride at the exact same pace as the guy in front of me.

I like riding in the back so much that I rode behind Mike most of the way to Alaska and back. I think he preferred it that way.

There is a problem with this concept, however.

There's only one slot in the back.

ONE HUNDRED TWELVE

Turn Right to Somewhere

One Spring morning, while out for a ride, I decided to turn right on a road I had never noticed. I'd probably never been on this road because it wasn't the quickest way to anywhere. I was ten miles from home.

As I crested the first hill, the landscape changed.

Rolling pastures and old barns replaced commercial buildings and four-lane highways. Trees covered sections of the road and leaves cast shadows over the newly poured asphalt.

The road was far from straight, which made it even better.

I imagine this road was first made when property lines were more important than straight lines. I couldn't believe this place existed so close to my home—and that I had never even noticed.

This isn't the only unusual road I've uncovered nearby.

On another day, I rode north into Tennessee on the smallest road I could find. In no time, I felt like I had gone back in time.

Pastures were popping with spring grass, and cattle seemed to be enjoying the warmth of spring and the abundance of food. Simple roads led to simple homes that reminded me of my grandparent's farm.

Every farmhouse had a barn. I saw tractors, plows, cultivators, and hay bailers. This took me back to my childhood when my grandfather would let me drive his tractor to move bales of hay.

It felt like I was going back in time—but in a good way.

When I don't have a place I must go, I turn down roads I've never been. And more often than not, they lead me to places that rejuvenate my soul. Sometimes, the best rides are the ones without a plan.

The next time you don't have somewhere to be, take a chance.

———

And turn right to nowhere.

I Had to Lay-er-Down

Many years ago, I met a man at a neighborhood dinner party who had just wrecked his motorcycle. Bob looked rough. His right arm was broken, his chin was heavily bandaged, and his walk was strained.

Bob was the center of attention as he *proudly* told his story.

"I was on Highway 72 (a four-lane) traveling east. I was in the left lane going around two slower cars. Without warning, the second car pulled into my lane right in front of me. To keep from hitting him, I grabbed my rear brake with everything I had."

With pride, he continued:

"I had to lay-er-down."

Later that night in private, I asked Bob more about his accident. I let him do most of the talking. After listening to part of his story, I asked, "How much front brake did you use?"

He looked surprised at my question and quickly answered, *"None."*

By now, you know that Bob lowsided because he locked up his rear tire. You also know that if Bob would have had ABS, he wouldn't have lowside crashed that day.

BUT PERHAPS THE MOST TROUBLING THING ABOUT ALL THIS WAS BOB'S FAILURE TO USE HIS FRONT BRAKE—AT ALL.

When confronted with a crash, Bob chose to use his rear brake, something that's so ineffective at doing what its title suggests, that he ended up skidding to a stop on his butt—which is even less effective.

My mentor Pete, an experienced rider coach, once told me that the only viable reason he could come up with for *laying-er-down* would be to slide under a tractor-trailer.

He's right. *Laying-er-down* is never a wise decision.

I've always said that being a good rider starts with head knowledge. And the first thing a rider should put in their head about motorcycles is that they stop quicker with their front brake.

Bob moved away a short time later. I hope he stopped riding.

Bob, I should have been more vocal about telling you all this. But somehow, I didn't think you wanted to hear what I had to say. You seemed so proud of yourself. For me to say your wounds could have been avoided seemed heartless. But looking back, NOT at least trying was a failure on my part, and I'm sorry. —David

It's stories like this that have given me the clarity to champion the USE YOUR FRONT BRAKE mantra—that you may have noticed (sincerely) throughout this book.

Part Seven: Wrap-Up

I chuckle every time I think about my original plan for this book to be super short. I guess I had more to say than I thought I did.

In this section, I'll wrap things up and put a bow on it.

I'll also share what I call *The Motorcycle Smarts Creed*.

Stay with me. You're in the home stretch.

Riding in the Rain for the First Time

Weather predictions for the day showed a zero percent chance of rain.

Great, I think I'll ride my motorcycle to work.

The morning ride to work was everything a spring morning should be—cool and crisp with shades of fresh green all around.

Then, there was the ride home.

I left for home well before the late evening rain chances began—or so the weatherwoman said. Upon mounting my bike, I noticed the sky looked ominously dark in the direction of home.

I took a deep breath, zipped both zippers on my two-hour waterproof riding jacket, put the rain cover over my tank bag, and wrapped my finger squeegee on my left pointer finger.

It didn't take me long to realize that I was about to get wet. At that moment, I wished I had practiced riding in the rain like Fred said.

My predictions proved to be true.

About one mile into my ten-mile trip, the rain began. I leaned over my tank and ducked behind my shield as low as I could go.

Perfect, the rain was barely hitting my helmet.

The rain steadily increased, and my speed decreased due to traffic. Unfortunately, ducking no longer provided the desired relief.

My Honda riding jacket that was supposed to be waterproof for up to two hours either had a problem at the manufacturing facility in Indonesia, or they never tested the jacket in this type of wet.

Within minutes, I felt moisture wicking into my clothes.

But that was the least of my problems.

My finger squeegee worked as designed, and I was able to free my left hand periodically to wipe the outside of my shield. But managing the fog on the *inside* of the shield proved to be more challenging.

I'm confident holding my breath would have helped. But as you might expect, I was breathing faster than normal.

My only choice was to open my face shield slightly, allowing air to circulate around the *inside* of my helmet. This trick effectively reduced the fog but introduced other problems.

Water poured down the inside of my shield onto my tank bag, and from there onto my jeans and into my riding boots.

It was raining so hard the roads were overwhelmed with standing water. Regardless of how far I tried to distance myself from the cars around me, I was catching muck and road grime in all directions.

I knew they couldn't help it.

The most uncomfortable sensations came as water flowed from my motorcycle seat into my most delicate of parts. Water ran from rear to front (surprisingly) until the area was completely saturated.

The evaporative cooling effect of the wind and the moisture only exacerbated the already compromising situation.

My Honda Interceptor temperature gauge read 50F, yet my glove-soaked hands felt frozen—as did the rest of my wet body parts.

During most of my commute home, I was cold and miserable. I must have looked like something sharp was attached to my seat.

I was puckered as puckered could be. I couldn't help but notice drivers around me staring. I tried to stay tucked below my windscreen in hopes of avoiding every drop of water I could manage.

It wasn't working so well.

THEN SOMETHING CHANGED

About halfway through my ten-mile ride home, something changed in my head. I went from loathing the moment to enjoying it.

At that moment, I sat straight up and started laughing.

This is just like camping or splashing in the rain when I was a kid, I thought. No. This is actually better.

I smiled at folks around me as if to say,

"This must look funny, but I'm having the time of my life."

I felt vulnerable and amazingly lucky. In the car on my left, there were kids in the back seat pointing at me. I took my left hand off the left grip for long enough to wave and smile back.

They understood why I was having fun. I felt like a kid again.

When I pulled into my garage, I couldn't help but laugh.

"That was freaking amazing."

It's hard to describe the moment. I felt richer for the experience—just like I did on all the campouts that didn't go exactly as planned.

Except this time, I appreciated what happened before it was over. That's what a few more years of life under my belt brings to the table.

Later that night, I remembered my rain pants were in my tank bag.

Oh well.

IF YOU HAVEN'T RIDDEN IN THE RAIN, YOU'VE MISSED OUT ON ONE OF THE MOST JOYOUS THINGS YOU CAN DO ON TWO WHEELS.

Use Your Front Brake—A Final Reminder

I've noticed in the last several years that if you tell me fifty things to remember, I won't remember a single one of them.

If, on the other hand, you give me a handful of strong points—repeated in an easy, fun way—I'll remember all of them.

That's been one of my hat tricks for the Motorcycle Smarts book series.

So much so that I almost titled this book, *Use Your Front Brake*.

The concept is so simple. Folks just need to be convinced of it.

So, I'll say it one last time. Using your front brake is the *only* right way to brake in normal on-street situations.

And if you've mostly been using your rear brake, the best way to fix that is to start using your front brake *every time you ride*. The way you practice is the way you'll do it in a panic—when it counts most.

While I'm talking about braking, let me say it again.

MOSTLY USING YOUR REAR BRAKE IS A BAD IDEA BECAUSE IT DOESN'T WORK VERY WELL, AND A LOCKED-UP REAR TIRE (super easy to do without ABS) TRIGGERS MOST LOWSIDE AND HIGHSIDE CRASHES.

Your rear brake isn't very effective and can be dangerous without ABS. A potentially deadly combination.

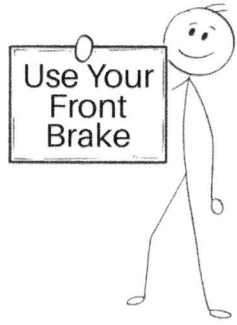

The Motorcycle Smarts Creed

I wrote this to help me get into the right mindset before I ride. It's called the *Motorcycle Smarts Creed*.

> *I will only ride my motorcycle on this day if my mind is clear, my body is rested, and my soul is undistracted.*
>
> *Today, I will focus on improving my riding skills. I will practice doing what I do well and what I don't do so well.*
>
> *I will ride defensively and assume others don't see me. I will watch closely for distracted drivers and give them extra space.*
>
> *I will position myself so others can see me and ride at a comfortable pace, even if this means I arrive at my destination a few minutes late.*
>
> *I will represent the motorcycling community to the best of my abilities. I will wave to every motorcyclist, regardless of what they're riding.*
>
> *I will stay focused on the tasks before me. I will remain*

*patient and expect nothing from the drivers around
me. If someone does something stupid, I will not blow
a fuse, make a hand gesture, or yell inside my helmet.*

*I will notice the beauty of nature around me. I will appre-
ciate the smells of changing seasons and the uniqueness
of every cloud. I will enjoy the warmth of the sun
shining on me, and the different shades of green
Mother Nature has painted for me.*

*And when my ride is done, and my thoughts are clear, I
will document today in my journal—the good, the
bad, and the silent thoughts that pop into my head
only when I ride.*

Because today is a special day.

Just Three Things

At the end of the day, I recognize that I won't be able to change every reader's mind. But I do want to make a difference.

Some have already brushed me off as crazy because I encouraged them to use their front brake over their rear—and told the truth that LOUD PIPES DON'T SAVE LIVES.

But honestly, these folks were never my target audience.

My strategy throughout this book was to present a case for how a *few* changes could make a measurable difference in the crash data.

Sure, I did this at the cost of repetition—but that was my ploy.

Consider this. I believe if you do three things, you can significantly reduce your chances of crashing. Of course, you could do more, but I'm back to my theory that if I tell you three things, you're much more likely to remember them than if I tell you fifteen.

Here, I'll make a case for three things that could change the crash data.

1. Riders need to use their front brake.

To make this happen, riders need to be educated on the DANGERS of *failing* to use their front brake—and the DANGERS of *overusing* (locking up) their rear brake.

Teaching this to beginning riders is enormously more important than helping them select a helmet or riding jacket. So why don't we?

The instructor in my first MSF course didn't say a thing about the dangers of locking up my rear tire. Nothing.

ONE OF THE BIGGEST CATALYSTS FOR THIS BOOK SERIES WAS THAT I WANTED TO EXPLAIN LOWSIDE AND HIGHSIDE CRASHES IN A SIMPLE TO UNDERSTAND WAY.

Specifically, I wanted to show how ABS could virtually eliminate these crashes—which are almost always rider-induced. I figured if I could explain why ABS is so important, I could effect change.

I'm still baffled that the subject of lowside and highside crashes is mostly brushed over in the most popular motorcycle mega-books.

If they hadn't been, I doubt I would have written a single book.

2. Riders should ride motorcycles with ABS.

My preference would be that it has Traction Control or Stability Control too. But those can be harder to find on some bikes.

And the best way for this to happen is for ABS (at a minimum) to be federally mandated on all on-street motorcycles sold in the U.S.

While Congress is going through the process, they should mandate Stability Control too. Congress mandated ABS and Electronic Stability Control on cars and light trucks back in 2012.

These electronics are even more important on motorcycles.

What are you waiting for?

To keep everyone happy, mandate that they can be cut off so riders can disengage the systems when they don't want them.

3. RIDERS SHOULD WEAR BRIGHT GEAR.

This one is obvious, but hi-vis yellow might not be your thing.

I've gone through all the data, and it's clear that one of the biggest reasons motorists hit us is because they don't *see* us.

So, the obvious fix is for us to wear stuff that makes us easy to see.

And if you think a flashing taillight is enough, you're mistaken.

Bright riding gear (along with a bright helmet) will cut the chances a motorist will turn left across your lane and hit you, which is a significant percentage of all multi-vehicle crashes.

My point here is simple. Changing even a few things can measurably reduce a rider's chances of crashing.

Think of it this way. Even if I preached about helmets, I doubt a single person would ever contact me and say, "Thanks, Dave. I'm glad you suggested I wear a helmet—cause I had no idea they could help."

But occasionally, I DO have riders contact me and say,

"I got a motorcycle with ABS because you explained why it matters."

And when I get those emails, I smile for the rest of the day.

I'm the *use your front brake, choose ABS, wear bright gear* guy.

Simple as that.

Wait a second. I have something else.

It's called the *Motorcycle Smarts* Quick Tip Newsletter—and every rider should sign up to receive it.

Honestly, to sign up NOW might be the best tip in this book.

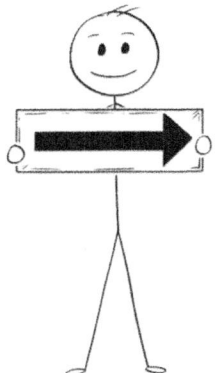

"Motorcycle Smarts" Quick Tips Newsletter

Free weekly riding tips you can consume in less than 3 minutes— delivered to your inbox for you to use and share with others.

motorcyclesmarts.com/tips

You're not doing everything you can to keep from crashing until you're signed up.

Sign up at the link below. Unsubscribe at any time.
motorcyclesmarts.com/tips

Final Thoughts

When I set out to write the first book in this series, *Motorcycle Smarts*, I was motivated by the data in the Hurt Report to do something to help riders understand how motorcycles work—and why they crash.

Years later, when I started looking at the crash data for this book, I quickly learned that nothing has changed.

It sure would be more comfortable to blame the distracted driver who pulled out in front of us or the drunken driver who swerved into our lane. But that's only a *fraction* of what's causing us to crash.

The data doesn't lie.

From all my research, I believe Hurt was right when he said that riders are making the same mistakes we did forty years ago.

We're killing ourselves in single-vehicle crashes by refusing to learn how motorcycles work and why they crash.

Riders are still crashing because they aren't using their front brake; they don't understand what happens when they lock up their rear tire, and because they don't know what to do when going wide in a turn.

Riders are
making the same
mistakes we did
forty years ago.

If you ride a motorcycle, the burden is on your shoulders to learn how to control it. Unfortunately, wearing a helmet won't help with that. Neither will riding a motorcycle with loud pipes.

Am I suggesting we can reduce our risks to zero? No.

Skilled riders crash and die every day when there was nothing they could have done to prevent (or avoid) it.

BUT IT'S ALSO TRUE THAT UNDER-SKILLED RIDERS CRASH AND DIE EVERY DAY WHEN THERE was SOMETHING THEY COULD HAVE DONE TO AVOID IT.

If I didn't think I could measurably reduce my chances of being in a crash, I wouldn't ride. I believe you can reduce your chances too.

MASTERING THE ART OF RIDING A MOTORCYCLE WELL is about learning how to ride the right way. It's about taking each ride seriously. It's about enjoying the experience and making good decisions based on the laws of physics.

It's about being confident you can avoid distracted drivers. It's about having a plan before you need a plan. It takes effort.

It's about understanding and overcoming rider fear, and having the head knowledge of how your motorcycle works so you can make it go where you want it to go. It's about understanding why riders crash.

Learning how to control your motorcycle should be your primary goal when you buy your first motorcycle, or your next goal if you've ridden for decades.

Control is the skill that makes you less likely to be in an accident. It's the path to proficient riding.

My Final Challenge

As our time together comes to an end, I leave you with the same challenge I did in *Motorcycle Smarts*—to BE INTENTIONAL.

Be intentional about learning how to ride more proficiently, intentional about taking steps to reduce your risks, and intentional about wearing the proper riding gear.

Don't be the gal that says there's nothing you can do to ride safer. Don't be the guy that says you can't reduce your risks. Don't be the one who doesn't know about the Hurt Report, what countersteering does, or why you should never lock up your rear tire.

Don't be the guy who doesn't wear a helmet because his buddies think helmets aren't cool.

Instead, take each ride seriously and learn something new about you and your motorcycle every time you ride. Keep a journal. Document what you did well and what you need to work on next.

Choose who you ride with like your life depends on it. It does.

Find a motorcycle that fits your body and your riding goals.

BE EXTRA CAREFUL OF DRIVERS TURNING LEFT ACROSS YOUR LANE. RIDERS CRASH AND DIE EVERY DAY WHEN THIS HAPPENS.

Assume motorists can't see you because sometimes they simply can't—especially if you're wearing dull colors.

Know how to use countersteering to put your motorcycle exactly where you want it, regardless of how small you are and how large it is.

Consider buying a motorcycle with ABS because the advantages of ABS far outweigh the disadvantages.

Practice in all types of weather conditions so you'll be ready when it happens in real life. Don't be the guy who brags:

"My motorcycle has never seen the rain."

Always leave margin so you're not pressured to ride faster than you planned to. Take a ride to nowhere just because you can. Explore roads near your home that you've never taken.

Take the long way to familiar places.

Don't get ahead of your skills. Save the cross-country trip for later. Ditto for riding Deals Gap until you're sure you can handle it.

Be intentional about taking hands-on training because nothing can take its place (not even this book series). Practice your craft often.

Believe you can reduce your chances of crashing because you can.

Use rider fear as a motivator to improve your riding skills or as a sign you should choose a different craft.

Know what to do when you start going wide in a turn and how to keep from lowsiding and highsiding.

Read the Hurt Report and listen to what it teaches us.

Represent the riding community well by being courteous and cool. What one of us does reflects on all of us, whether we like it or not.

Wait three seconds after the light turns green before going.

WEAR BRIGHT COLORS. Avoid riding at night.

Choose loud pipes if you want to. Just don't ask them to save you. Lazy solutions rarely work.

 **Don't lock up your rear tire because bad things happen when you do.**

And the simplest way to keep from locking up your rear tire is to ride a motorcycle with ABS. *Why is this even controversial?* Even better, ride one that has Traction Control and Stability Control, too.

Never buy a motorcycle until there's margin in your finances.

Look where you want to go because that's where you're going.

Treat every intersection like it's one of the most dangerous things you do on a motorcycle—because it is.

Know when to call it quits, and have the courage to do it *boldly*.

Choose your riding friends carefully.

Never ride when you're not at your best.

Leave margin at all times. Then call on it to save your life.

Be super careful riding in gravel. It's like walking on marbles.

Never be somewhere a motorist might want to go.

Ride at your own pace. Choose your riding partners carefully.

Wave to all riders, regardless of what they're riding or whether you think they'll wave back.

And lastly, the easiest takeaway from this entire book.

Use your front brake.
Use your front brake.
USE YOUR FRONT BRAKE!

MASTERING THE ART OF RIDING WELL is a journey not a destination. Ask any experienced rider who's been doing this for decades, and they'll tell you they never stop learning.

I learn something about myself every time I ride. That's one of the best things about motorcycles — there's always something left to learn, something left to experience, something left to ask yourself.

Remember what the store clerk said to Mike and me in Colorado before we headed out to ride the Million Dollar Highway? I hear her words inside my helmet every time I suit up to ride.

"RIDERS CRASH AND DIE EVERY WEEK ON THE STRETCH OF ROAD YOU GUYS ARE ABOUT TO RIDE."

If you're just starting out, my best advice is to enjoy the journey.

Just like you remember your college days as your best years, you'll look back on the journey of selecting, buying, and outfitting your first motorcycle as a special time in your life. Trust me, I remember.

I'm telling you this now, so you can appreciate the process.

Don't stress out so much. Enjoy every moment.

You'll never take your first ride in the rain again.

You'll never ride on an interstate for the first time again.

You'll never ride to Alaska for the first time ever again.

So what if you don't like the bike you just bought in six months?

So what if you wished you'd purchased a different riding jacket?

My first motorcycle had an engine noise that concerned me. I obsessed over it trying to figure out what it was, thinking the guy had sold it to me with a known problem. I later discovered it was a normal characteristic of that particular overhead cam engine.

I regret wasting all that energy and emotion.

The Finish Line Is Near

Of all the topics in this book, there's one that resonates most.

My mentor Fred stopped riding when he was the age I am now.

And Fred is a wise man.

In the end, Fred stopped riding when he felt like it was time. And I will do the same thing.

During the last several months while writing this book, I've been thinking a lot about when it might be the right time to stop riding.

My kids are now past their teenage years and sometimes impart wisdom to me. My son was right when he told me just the other day:

"Dad, you need to be bold in deciding when to stop riding—instead of letting your motorcycle sit in the garage and fade away."

Drew was right. I know it's time.

I've decided that once I complete this book, I'm going to sell my motorcycle (the same one I rode to Alaska on) and stop riding.

This is my decision, and it's *not* based on fear. It's based on a risk-to-reward formula in my mind that I've talked about before. This has nothing to do with my age. It has everything to do with my gut.

As a confirmation of this decision, just last week while driving, I failed to yield correctly at a traffic light and turned left—right in front of someone coming my way. The motorist slammed on his brakes and barely missed me. I was fortunate he didn't have a gun. He was upset!

It wasn't until the next day that I realized that this was the exact thing Fred was looking for to signal it was time for him to stop riding. I had my confirmation that it's time to choose a different craft.

This amazing journey that began for me at forty when I bought my first real motorcycle is now finished.

This book completes my journey.

I'll say to you what Fred said to me. *"It's been a good ride."*

Thank you all for following along and reading what I had to say about something I fell in love with when my parents reluctantly agreed to let me purchase a 1973 bright orange Honda Express moped.

In the basement of my house back in 2007, I pulled out a perfectly typed set of notes ten pages long and placed it in front of my motorcycle mentors. With more confidence than I deserved, I proclaimed:

"Someday, I'm going to explain motorcycles my way."

In my wildest imagination, I had no idea I would end up here.

My six-inch stack of notes that was the foundation for this book is now less than one inch thick. Regardless of what I do with this pile, I feel like I've accomplished what I promised my mentors I would do.

I'VE EXPLAINED MOTORCYCLES MY WAY.

In a deeply personal way, writing these final words feels amazing.

"I finished what I started" feels pretty darn good.

Thank you again for following along.

I'm honored you were here.

To Fred and Pete. Thank you both for being my motorcycle mentors. It's probably safe to say that the 'Motorcycle Smarts' book series would have never materialized without your guidance in the early days. Hopefully, this book series will serve as a way to help riders long past when the three of us are gone.

How Can I Help?

My goal in writing the *Motorcycle Smarts* series was never financial.

Even though I've stopped riding, I'm passionate about the sport. If someone wants to champion mandatory ABS on all street motorcycles, I'd be happy to do what I can to help.

I'm also open to sharing parts of the unique content I wrote about in my books with online and print publications—especially the parts about lowside and highside crashes.

Thanks again for following along. —*David*

david@motorcyclesmarts.com
linkedin.com/in/david-mixson/

Courtesy Copies for Rider Coaches

My vision has always been to share this book with as many folks as possible. That's my best shot at changing the crash data.

I'd like to start by sending a free copy of this book to as many rider coaches as I can. My hope is that every coach might find a nugget of useful information that they can share with their students—possibly on the topic of what triggers lowside and highside crashes.

Just a suggestion.

But I don't want to stop there.

If I can get enough company sponsorships and individual support, I'd like to provide free/discounted copies to riding clubs and rallies.

Learn more about the *Motorcycle Smarts Dream Team* below.

I can't do this alone.

motorcyclesmarts.com/dreamteam

Appendix

In this final section, I'll introduce my mentors, tell you what folks are saying about the *Motorcycle Mentor Podcast,* and give you a sneak peek at the other books in the *Motorcycle Smarts* book series.

And lastly, I'll ask for your help.

Meet My Motorcycle Mentors

I was lucky. I found two men willing to help me when I started riding. Their guidance was less about how to ride the correct way and more about the mental steps you must take to become a proficient rider.

Let's meet them.

Fred Applegate

Fred and I worked together at NASA in the late '90s training astronauts for Spacelab flights and controlling science experiments onboard the Space Shuttle.

Fred retired when he was still young and in good health. In his free time, he played golf, took tennis lessons, and continued enjoying his lifelong passion for riding his Honda ST1100.

Fred is very methodical, detail-oriented, disciplined, cautious, and patient. When I started toying with the idea of buying a motorcycle, I immediately approached him for guidance.

Fred agreed to become my motorcycle mentor.

He graciously helped me through every new challenge. Instead of giving me the answer to my problem, he always guided me toward the solution—knowing it would mean more if I figured it out for myself. *Fred was the perfect mentor.*

Pete Tamblyn

Pete was one of the top motorcycle instructors in the country.

If you've taken a Stayin' Safe Advanced Motorcycle Training class, Pete might have been your instructor. Over the years, Pete has helped thousands of riders as an instructor at several different riding schools.

Lucky for me, Pete and Fred were roommates back in college and good friends today. Fred refers to Pete as *his* motorcycle mentor. Pete was gracious with his time and always answered my toughest questions with patience and thoroughness.

UPDATE: During the final edits of this book, Pete emailed me.

"I just recently sold my last full capable motorcycle—a white 2021 650 V-Strom. The last thing I want to do is limp off into the sunset, wishing I had known when to quit but had instead kept riding a bike which had become too unwieldy for my aging frame. I cried a little that day but stuck with my plan and took the nice man's money and helped him tie her down on his trailer. Jackie still rides with me on the Can-Am, which isn't a motorcycle but is still enjoyable if we keep the right mindset. I smile that I'm content these days to entertain the bright little faces of two young granddaughters lots of weekends and spend the rest of my spare time writing my memoirs and meeting some friends at the gym. Being 82 isn't all that bad." —Pete

GENTLEMEN. THANK YOU AGAIN. THIS WORLD NEEDS MORE MENTORS LIKE YOU.

Would You Help?

I'd like to thank you for purchasing my book. You could have picked from dozens of other resources, but you took a chance to hear what I had to say. I'm honored.

Before you go, can I ask you for a favor?

If you found the information in this book useful and think other riders could benefit from reading it, would you please write an honest review on Amazon? It's because if this book doesn't consistently receive positive reviews, it won't show up when riders search for help.

I really want this to be a "five-star" quality book.

Thank you for doing this.

P.S. If you've written a review for any of my other books
in the 'Motorcycle Smarts' series. Thank you so much!

More 'Motorcycle Smarts' Books

Motorcycle Smarts: Overcome Fear, Learn Control, Master Riding Well

Motorcycle Smarts is the first book in the *Motorcycle Smarts* book series. Do you feel *guilty* for wanting to ride a motorcycle?

Do you have a *fear* that overcomes you when you ride?

Do you want to enjoy the *peace of mind* knowing that you're doing everything possible NOT to crash?

Riders crash and die every day in RIDER-INDUCED CRASHES —and it doesn't have to be this way.

In addition to in-depth discussions about rider fear and how not to crash, *Motorcycle Smarts* tackles important topics like *countersteering*, *muscle memory*, and *braking*.

It also goes over some of the most important lessons from the Hurt Report and makes a case for only riding motorcycles with ABS.

You won't find page-filling discussions about bike rallies and riding gear. Instead, you'll find the most in-depth explanation of lowside and highside crashes that exists anywhere.

Here's what one reader said:

"I've read 'Total Control,' 'Proficient Motorcycling,' and 'Stayin Safe,' but the section in 'Motorcycle Smarts' on lowside and highside crashes is all the difference. David is great at simplifying difficult concepts. I'm definitely passing along this book to my riding friends."

— Dano in San Diego, California

Mastering the art of riding well is about understanding and over-coming *fear*. It's about having the *head knowledge of how your motorcycle works* so you can make it go where you want it to go.

It's about *taking ownership of your riding safety.*

For more information visit:
motorcyclesmarts.com/books

Motorcycle Dream Ride: My Alabama to Alaska Adventure

Motorcycle Dream Ride is the second book in the series.

This book documents the journey from Alabama to Alaska I made with my best friend, Mike.

Motorcycle Dream Ride isn't just for motorcyclists. It's for anyone who dreams of doing something magical but gets stuck in excuses and self-doubts. It's for anyone who needs encouragement to do that *something* they've always dreamed of doing but haven't.

I wrote ride reports at the end of each day and shared them online. But I didn't reveal everything that happened.

I didn't share the self-doubts going through my mind when Mike and I pulled out of my driveway.

And I didn't introduce the people we met along the way.

This book doesn't just document our trip. It peels back the layers and exposes what we discovered along the way about life, about adversity, and about living our big dream.

Here's what readers have said:

"This book is about more than motorcycles. It's about friendship and living life to the fullest. David and Mike, thank you for documenting your journey so we could follow along."

— Danielle in Kentucky

"I loved this book. I started reading it last night and wouldn't go to bed until I finished it. Now I'm working on answering David's challenge questions. David has always been a favorite writer of mine."

— Chris in Wrightstown, Pennsylvania

Riding to somewhere far away has been on my bucket list for a very long time—and I finally did it.

The ride changed the way I look at life.

And I'd love to tell you how.

For more information visit:
motorcyclesmarts.com/books

The Motorcycle Mentor Podcast

I started the *Motorcycle Mentor Podcast* to help riders at all levels learn how motorcycles work—and why they crash. You can listen for FREE on iTunes, Stitcher, Overcast, Apple TV, Pocket Casts, Amazon Music, iHeartRadio, or any of your favorite podcast channels.

The podcast has been downloaded more than 250,000 times. *I'm truly honored!*

Here's what listeners are saying ...

"Hello, David. When I was in my MSF course, a funny thing happened. I recognized a reference my rider coach made as being from your show. This surprised me at first, but it turns out that Kevin and I are both fans. You have fans all over the country, even here in small-town Vermont."

— Jeff Green in Randolph, VT

*"So thankful I found this podcast.
David is personable, humble, and knowledgeable."*

— NMcClure via iTunes

"Invaluable insights. I discovered this podcast shortly after passing my MSF course. I've been following David since he first started broadcasting and have found his insights and suggestions absolutely invaluable."

— CoopBMT via iTunes

"A MUST LISTEN for any rider!"

— Brent Boxall via iTunes

"On a technical level, the audio quality is good, and the host is always on topic. It is obvious that he puts a lot of work into each episode before hitting the record button. There is no stream-of-consciousness rambling like you get when you try to watch motorcycle reviews on YouTube. Riding a motorcycle is a serious endeavor, and this show is a great resource."

— Highlander 357 via iTunes

"I rode a bike many years ago. Now at 60, I'm returning to ride. The Motorcycle Mentor Podcast is a good find. I looked around for other podcasts and got a few that sounded like guys sitting around the coffee table with a tape recorder running and just BS-ing. Being an engineer, David isn't afraid to throw in a touch of physics. Not math, though."

— CoopBMT via iTunes

"I mentor new riders, and your podcast is an instant recommendation. David, you will never know how many lives you saved."

"I recently completed my MSF class. But this podcast has given me the tools to be an even better rider. Thank you."

David Here ...

I'll tell you this upfront. I don't have a radio voice, but I do have the heart of a teacher. I work hard to make each show informative and to the point. If you enjoyed this book, I think you'll like the podcast.

I strive to make the show a "five-star" quality podcast.

You can learn more about the podcast at:
motorcyclesmarts.com/podcast

Notes

A Fresh Approach

1. National Highway Traffic Safety Administration, "2012 Data: Motorcycles," NHTSA, June 2014, https://crashstats.nhtsa.dot.gov/Api/Public/ViewPublication/812035.
2. National Highway Traffic Safety Administration, "Motorcycle Safety," NHTSA, accessed December 1, 2022, https://www.nhtsa.gov/road-safety/motorcycles.

Chapter Eight

1. Umesh Shankar, "Fatal Single Vehicle Motorcycle Crashes," National Center for Statistics and Analysis, Publication No. DOT HS 809 360, October 2001, https://rosap.ntl.bts.gov/view/dot/6426.

Chapter Eleven

1. Hugh H. Hurt, J. V. Ouellet, David R. Thom, *Motorcycle Accident Cause Factors and Identification of Countermeasures. Volume 1 Technical Report* (Los Angeles: National Highway Traffic Safety Administration, 1981), https://rosap.ntl.bts.gov/view/dot/6450.

Chapter Fifteen

1. Motorcycle Cruiser, "Effective Braking - Street Survival," February 24, 2009, https://www.motorcyclecruiser.com/effective-braking-street-survival/.

Chapter Twenty-Six

1. David L. Hough, "Interview With Harry Hurt," Sound RIDER, accessed December 1, 2022, https://soundrider.com/archive/safety-skills/harry_hurt_interview.aspx.

Chapter Twenty-Eight

1. Zhenyu Wang, Chanyoung Lee, and Pei-Sung Lin, "Study on Motorcycle Safety in Negotiation with Horizontal Curves in Florida and Development of Crash Modification Factors," *Center for Urban Transportation Research*, October 2018, https://fdotwww.blob.core.windows.net/sitefinity/docs/default-source/research/reports/fdot-bdv25-977-21-rpt.pdf?sfvrsn=c892003f_2.

Chapter Forty

1. Sally Kalson, "Obituary: Lawrence Grodsky / Top American Expert on Motorcycle

Safety," *Pittsburgh Post-Gazette,* April 11, 2006, https://www.post-gazette.com/news/obituaries/2006/04/11/Obituary-Lawrence-Grodsky-Top-American-expert-on-motorcycle-safety/stories/200604110210.

Chapter Forty-Three
1. Hugh H. Hurt, J. V. Ouellet, David R. Thom, *Motorcycle Accident Cause Factors and Identification of Countermeasures. Volume 1 Technical Report* (Los Angeles: National Highway Traffic Safety Administration, 1981), https://rosap.ntl.bts.gov/view/dot/6450.

Chapter Forty-Five
1. The Hurt Report suggests riders don't understand lowside and highside crashes. Not because riders answered a poll and said they didn't, but because their actions crashing showed they didn't. The word "most" is my personal interpretation of the data.

Chapter Fifty
1. Blake Conner, "Off-Road Braking Test!," Cycle World, accessed December 1, 2022, https://www.cycleworld.com/2014/01/17/off-road-braking-test-pro-level-off-road-racer-against-ktm-abs/.

Chapter Fifty-One
1. Traction Control in MotoGP, "Valentino Rossi," accessed December 1, 2022, https://tractioncontrolinmotogp.weebly.com/valentino-rossi.html.

Chapter Fifty-Two
1. Jost Gail, Joachim Funke, Patrick Seiniger, and Ulrich Westerkamp, "Anti Lock Braking and Vehicle Stability Control for Motorcycles-Why or Why Not" (Proceedings of the 21st ESV Conference, Stuttgart, Germany, Paper Number 09-0072, 15–18 June 2009), https://smarter-usa.org/wp-content/uploads/2017/12/17.-2009-Anti-lock-Braking-and-Vehicle-Stability-Control-for-Motorcycles-Why-or-Why-Not.pdf.

Chapter Seventy-Seven
1. Motorcycle Cruiser, "12 Motorcycle Safety Myths and Misconceptions," February 24, 2009, https://www.motorcyclecruiser.com/12-motorcycle-safety-myths-and-misconceptions/.

Chapter Seventy-Nine
1. James R. Davis, "Brakes Their Real Job Is NOT to Stop - It Is to Slow the Bike," Motorcycle Tips and Techniques, accessed December 1, 2022, https://www.msgroup.org/Tip.aspx?Num=064.

CHAPTER EIGHTY
1. Federal Highway Administration, "Motorcycle Crash Causation Study," Federal Highway Administration, Publication No. FHWA-HRT-18-064, February 2019, https://www.fhwa.dot.gov/publications/research/safety/18064/18064.pdf.

CHAPTER EIGHTY-TWO
1. David L. Hough, "Interview With Harry Hurt," Sound RIDER, accessed December 1, 2022, https://soundrider.com/archive/safety-skills/harry_hurt_in terview.aspx.

CHAPTER EIGHTY-THREE
1. Hugh H. Hurt, J. V. Ouellet, David R. Thom, *Motorcycle Accident Cause Factors and Identification of Countermeasures. Volume 1 Technical Report* (Los Angeles: National Highway Traffic Safety Administration, 1981), https://rosap.ntl.bts.gov/view/dot/6450.

CHAPTER EIGHTY-FOUR
1. Federal Highway Administration, "Motorcycle Crash Causation Study," Federal Highway Administration, Publication No. FHWA-HRT-18-064, February 2019, https://www.fhwa.dot.gov/publications/research/safety/18064/18064.pdf.

About the Author

I'm just a guy who fell in love with motorcycles.

David at the top of Pikes Peak in Colorado on the way
back from his dream ride to Alaska in 2015.

Hi. I'm David. I'm the author of the *Motorcycle Smarts* book series and host of the *Motorcycle Mentor Podcast*.

I begged my parents for a motorcycle when I was thirteen.

They said no, so I settled for an orange Honda Express moped.

I thought I'd died and gone to heaven the first time I rode it. Her top speed was only 35 mph (downhill), but that didn't stop me from exploring places far from home. If my parents only knew?

THE MOTORCYCLE HOOK WAS SET.

A Late Start

In 2005, nearly 27 years later, I purchased my first real motorcycle—a used Honda VFR. I was forty at the time. *Laugh here if you want.*

At forty-something, I approached my new passion with a certain level of maturity. I wanted to enjoy all the pleasures of riding, making friends, and exploring the unknown. But I wanted to do it the right way—with the right gear, the right skills, and the right mindset.

Like it was yesterday, I remember being overcome with fear the first time I rode it in traffic. I remember wondering if I was crazy for even thinking about owning a motorcycle. I remember feeling like my motorcycle was in control of me—instead of me being in control of it.

I consumed everything I could find about riding. I devoured every book I could get my hands on. I practiced what I learned.

And I found two generous men willing to mentor me.

A short time later, I created motorcyclementor.com and started the *Motorcycle Mentor Podcast.* More than a decade after that, I wrote the *Motorcycle Smarts* book series to share what I had learned.

What I Believe

I believe the physics of motorcycling gives us clues on how we can ride more safely. I'm a mechanical engineer, and I love dissecting how motorcycles work. I also enjoy taking complex ideas and making them simple to understand.

In 2022, I retired from NASA after 33 years as an engineer there.

I'm not a motorcycle instructor, but neither am I so far removed from the struggles beginning riders experience that I can't remember.

Michael Hyatt, New York Times best-selling author, said it best.

"Sometimes I think we can report best when we are newest to a task and the new hasn't rubbed off, and we still know what it takes to succeed or get started."

MOTORCYCLES FASCINATE ME. I LEARN SOMETHING NEW EVERY TIME I RIDE. AND I DON'T THINK THAT WILL EVER CHANGE.

Part geek, part engineer, part teacher—my passion is learning something new and teaching others what I discovered along the way.

I married my college sweetheart more than 30 years ago.

Sue and I have two children (Maddie and Drew) and three dogs (two Shih Tzus and a Great Dane).

---

*As I've said before, my purpose for writing the
'Motorcycle Smarts' book series was never financial.
If someone wants to champion mandatory ABS (and ESC)
on all street motorcycles, I'd be happy to do what I can to help.
Thanks again for following along.
—David*

david@motorcyclesmarts.com
linkedin.com/in/david-mixson/

Printed in Great Britain
by Amazon